AviaDossier #1

Canadian Aircraft of WWII

Text by Carl Vincent ©2007-2009

1st English Edition, SkyGrid ©2009

ISBN 978-0-9780696-3-6

Executive Editor • Terry Higgins

Editor • Elizabeth Vincent

Aircraft colour profiles and maps • Terry Higgins

All photos are from the author's collection unless credited otherwise. Where LAC or DND appear in a photo credit, they refer to Library and Archives Canada and Department of National Defence respectively.

Designed in Canada

Printed in China

Published in Canada

Aviaeology, by SkyGrid

123 Church Street

Kitchener, Ontario

Canada N2G 2S3

Fax: (519) 742-2182

Email: info@aviaeology.com

www.aviaeology.com

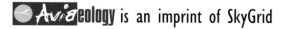 is an imprint of SkyGrid

Library and Archives Ca

Vincent, Carl, 1939-

    Canadian aircraft of WWII / text by Carl Vincent.

(AviaDossier ; #1)

Includes bibliographical references and index.

ISBN 978-0-9780696-3-6

1. Airplanes, Military--Canada--History.

2. Canada. Royal Canadian Air

Force--History--World War, 1939-1945.

3. World War, 1939-1945--Aerial

operations, Canadian.

I. Title. II. Series: AviaDossier #1

UG1245.C3V46 2009   358.4'1830971   C2009-902125-0

Contents

Canadian Aircraft of WWII

A New Aviaeology Series

This AviaDossier was initially conceived as a compact, yet comprehensive, showcase for author Carl Vincent's various and varied findings on the subject of *Canadian Aircraft of WWII*. During the research, dissemination and organization of historical material on the road to producing more comprehensive monograph-type works on many of the subject aircraft covered herein, it was realized that some of the nuggets thus sifted could, with a suitable shift in focus, be crafted into interesting narrative/pictorial essays. Something akin to the articles that appear in aviation history periodicals.

Front and centre for each is a narrative accompanied by a series of interesting photos. The focal point can vary greatly from subject to subject – an individual machine, an aircraft type as a whole, a noteworthy crew or pilot, a certain mission, etc. This content is rounded out with the addition of detailed colour profile illustrations worked up in close collaboration with the author and other researchers. Where possible, collateral findings on the more technical aspects of the subject aircraft – specific mission equipment, ordnance, finish and markings for example – are interlaced within the supporting captions adding yet another dimension to the overall package.

So that's basically it – variously focused articles as in periodical journals and magazines, packed with details on connected subjects as in a traditional dossier, all aviation related: *AviaDossier*.

Future volumes

AviaDossier #1 is intended as the first of several similar volumes each an exposé of *Canadian Aircraft of WWII*. It features 19 articles covering an eclectic array of aircraft types, missions, and personalities. These were shortlisted from a much larger master list originally presented by Mr. Vincent. It is truly surprising how many aircraft types the Royal Canadian Air Force employed during the Second World War. Time and again during this volume's preparation I was surprised to discover that the acquisition / introduction story for several aircraft types could easily compete with that of their service careers in terms of interest. Time and resources permitting, we intend to cover more subjects from that master list, offering similar depth and dimension, through at least one or two additional *AviaDossiers*.

Further, with this volume as our prototype, we'd like to offer *AviaDossier* as an occasional series covering other such collections of related subjects. We invite potential authors and researchers to contact us with prospective projects. Simply put, potential *AviaDossiers* should essay subjects – aircraft, operators, personalities – that have some obvious connection to each other and, it is hoped, offer some fresh perspective on at least some of them. If you've done some digging beyond what's currently in popular circulation, please feel free to get in touch with me at editor@aviaeology.com.

Terry Higgins

Kitchener, Ontario
9 March 2008

AviaDossier #1

Publisher's Note

Foreword

The Prime Minister of Canada, MacKenzie King, on 17 December 1939 in a radio broadcast to the Canadian people, described the British Commonwealth Air Training Plan (BCATP) as a co-operative undertaking of "great magnitude". The Plan was to train pilots initially and then aircrew of other types for overseas duty. For many, the plan was considered Canada's best war effort as it turned out 130,000 aircrew, of which 59,860 were pilots.

In addition to the BCATP and the Home War Establishment on national soil, Canada's war effort increased immensely with the formation of 48 operational squadrons overseas, that included eleven day fighter and three fighter-bomber squadrons of RCAF aircraft. All of these squadrons were numbered in the "400" block.

To me, as a young front line fighter pilot flying Kittyhawks on an RAF squadron in the African desert campaign, little or nothing was known of Canada's great effort back home. In fact, RCAF personnel seemed to be forgotten. Nonetheless, as members of RAF squadrons we were treated as equals and were quite content.

However, I had received my wings under the BCATP in June 1941 as a Sergeant Pilot and this was my first disappointment in the RCAF in that I wasn't commissioned. After 8 months on a RAF squadron I was leading the squadron as an NCO pilot one day when I shot down an Me109F. On return to base, the AOC who was visiting inquired "who was the successful pilot?" When he discovered that the leader was a Sergeant Pilot, he retorted, "Sergeant Pilots don't lead RAF squadrons!"

Following this I was interviewed by the Wing Commander for a commission in August 1942. However, some difficulty was experienced in getting it through RCAF channels so, consequently, I was commissioned from the ranks in the field to the rank of Flight Lieutenant by the RAF, befitting my position as Flight Commander on the squadron. To me this was a great honour.

After the war ended in North Africa in June 1943 I was sent back to El Ballah, near the Suez Canal, to help set up a gunnery school. In December of that same year I returned to ops with 417 Squadron RCAF in Italy on Spitfires as supernumerary. Two weeks later I joined 92 Squadron RAF as a Flight Commander and then I was given my own squadron – 274 Squadron RAF.

In April 1944 the squadron was posted back to England to bolster our air forces for the D-Day landings. As far as I knew RCAF HQ London wasn't aware of my return to "civilization" so in early July I checked in. My story could well apply to many RCAF personnel who served in the Middle East and the Far East on RAF units.

In August my squadron converted from Spitfires to Tempest aircraft to chase the V-1s. Soon after (September 1944) I was ordered back home to Canada. However, I returned overseas in March 1945, promoted to Wing Commander in charge of the four Spitfire squadrons of 127 Wing RCAF in Europe. As a Wing Commander Flying, I was entitled to have my initials, JFE, painted on my aircraft – kind of a recognition of achievement in the fighter pilot field. For me it was another great honour – from Sergeant Pilot to Wing Commander.

Busy as we were with operations and squadron movements, I was largely unaware of whatever we – Canadians, that is – were doing "back home". The BCATP and ongoing flow of RCAF overseas personnel notwithstanding, I don't recall ever having specific knowledge of the continued contribution that the RCAF Home War Establishment, or the Canadian aviation industry in general, were making towards the ongoing war effort. A good cross-section of such specifics, as well as interesting articles on the men and machines overseas, are aptly covered in this fine book.

Wing Commander (Ret.) JF Edwards, CM DFC & Bar, DFM, MID, CD

Comox, British Columbia
25 February 2008

Stocky Edwards getting reacquainted with the Curtiss Kittyhawk in 2005

photo: Jim Edwards via Pat Murphy of the Y2-K Spitfire project

Background: James Francis Edwards as a young Flight Lieutenant near the end of his desert war years.

Left: A little over one year and a nearly won war later, the still young Edwards returned to combat as Wing Commander Flying of 127 Wing RCAF after a short spell back in Canada.

photo: W/C J.F. "Stocky" Edwards

Preface

When Terry Higgins of Aviaeology persuaded me to indulge myself once more in the delights of military aviation research and writing after a hiatus of a couple of decades, he suggested this volume as an early project. After all, what could be more pleasant as an appetiser than a collection of short articles on an eclectic selection of Canadian aircraft of the Second World War with a few first-class photos and superb colour profiles for each? Not so much a teaser for the more solid works in preparation, both by myself and other authors, but a *smorgasbord*. A spread that would not only be attractive and whet the appetite for more, but would also contain solid, substantial and largely unfamiliar material.

Once decided, and without wanting to get hung up on definitions, there was still the question of what constituted a Canadian aircraft. Many of our non-Canadian readers (and, indeed, some of our Canadian ones) may not be aware of the fragmented nature of the RCAF during WWII. Even within a simplified description, there were in Canada both the Home War Establishment [HWE], which, at one time or another, operated 50 squadrons as well as smaller units, and the British Commonwealth Air Training Plan which, among its various establishments, contained nearly 100 schools and operational training units, each of which operated significant numbers of aircraft. However, though the RCAF administered and, to a large degree, operated and financed the Plan, the men and aircraft were a separate entity almost completely unavailable to the HWE. Overseas, there were, eventually, 47 RCAF squadrons. RCAF Overseas Headquarters had a certain and varying degree of control over these units, but, essentially they were under the operational command of the RAF. However 65 per cent, mainly aircrew, of RCAF personnel overseas did not even serve in RCAF units, but, rather in RAF units. In Ottawa, RCAF Headquarters kept an uneven and highly frustrated grasp on the reins of this mismatched quadriga.

In addition, there are two other categories that could be considered. A large number of Canadians had joined the RAF, mainly before the war, and many of these Can/RAF men were to have highly distinguished careers. Some transferred to the RCAF during and after the war. In addition there were two RAF squadrons, 242 (Canadian) and 125 (Newfoundland) in which an attempt was made for varying periods of time to concentrate RAF men from these respective dominions.

The aircraft the Canadians flew came from varied sources. The HWE units used aircraft obtained through pre-war contracts in Canada, the UK and the US, wartime contracts in Canada and the US, aircraft allotted from US production and paid for by Canada and even though Canada was not part of the Lend-Lease agreement, some Lend-Lease aircraft were received from the UK under exchange. All BCATP aircraft became the property of the administrator – Canada – and included not only Canadian aircraft obtained via all the above means but a large number of ex RAF and RN aircraft from British and American production. The RCAF units overseas were equipped by the RAF with RAF aircraft that remained RAF property as were those flown by Canadians in RAF units. There are inevitably numerous exceptions to all the above categories, several of which appear in this volume.

I eventually decided to include all aircraft owned by the RCAF including all HWE and Canadian-based BCATP types plus any aircraft flown by an RCAF unit anywhere. 242 and 125 RAF squadrons also qualify during relevant periods, though none of their aircraft were selected for this volume.

Why were these particular aircraft selected? I can only lay it to little more than rampant eclecticism. It was not, primarily, a choice because of interesting equipment, modifications or markings, although Canadian aircraft certainly do not take a back seat in that regard. The story will probably never be completely told concerning the multitude of variants of RCAF aircraft. As for the melange of prewar plus wartime versions of Canadian, British and American paint schemes as well as markings, all often applied with extreme individualism, it forms a fascinating study and a modeler's paradise.

I suppose some subjects were chosen because they seemed interesting at the time or I felt that the particular airframe was significant, e.g. the Sunderland, some because I was fed up with the erroneous information that had been published earlier, e.g. the Bolingbroke and Delta, or for which I had some great colour photos, e.g. the Stranraer and Shark. Some were selected because we had a run of photos illustrating the progressions of markings on a single airframe, e.g. the Hudson and Beaufighter. Others, because I was, for no conscious reason, thinking of them at the time. The depth of coverage also varies for no particular cause – simply what I then felt like writing. Some effort was made to provide a cross-section of types and operational location, but this is far from perfect. For example, there are no aircraft types from Bomber Command, though much of the RCAF's overseas effort was concentrated in this formation. The next volume in this series may well be weighted the other way.

Despite what may be viewed as an inconsistent approach to selection and treatment, I am confident that on examination this work will not be found wanting. The text is, I hope, logical and complete within the limits I have chosen for each subject. It is based, to an unusually high degree for a volume of this length, on primary source research and most sections contain information previously unpublished. The quality of the photos and profiles do not simply speak for themselves, but the accompanying captions are unusually comprehensive, complete and replete with new information. This total excellence is largely due to the talents of my colleague, publisher and illustrator, Terry Higgins. His insistence on accuracy, attention to detail and command of form and colour have resulted in profiles whose outstandingly high quality are apparent on first glance and truly amazing on close examination. His equivalent capacity to describe all this in a complete and readable fashion has helped create a happy combination of narrative text, description and illustration in this volume that approaches the unique. To return to the *smorgasbord* analogy, we present here a varied, interesting and unusual selection of illustrated essays designed not only to inform but to stimulate interest in Canadian aircraft of the Second World War.

Carl Vincent

Stittsville, Ontario
14 February 2009

Preface

Acknowledgements

As is usual with works of this nature, the content could not have come together as it did without the help of others.

Robert Bracken †	George Hopp
Steve Brooking	Ken Lawson
Buz Busby	Ross Marvin
Patrick Campbell	John Melson
Frank Cauley	Larry Milberry
Jerry Crandall	Pat Murphy
Jack Downey	Brian Musson
James "Stocky" Edwards	Ron Wylie, Wayne Ready, and Jack Frazier from CWHM, along with all the helpful guys on that museum's Bolingbroke project.
Kim Elliott	
Dave Fletcher	
Colin Ford	Mark Proulx
Jimmy Forrester †	Roger Sarty
Linda Fraser	Tony Stachiw
Stuart Fraser	Chris Thomas

As I indicated in the preface, this volume represents for me a return to this field of endeavour. Thus, a sizable percentage of the content was collected, though often not published, as much as a third of a century ago. It represents the contribution of, literally, hundreds of individuals, many of whom, alas, are no longer with us. Any attempt to recall and acknowledge them all after such a passage of time would, I fear, be more notable for omissions than inclusions. Therefore, I simply admit a debt of gratitude, far beyond my capacity to express, to these men and women.

I must also recognise those unsung heroes of the field of aviation history, the staffs of all the archives, museums and government organizations responsible for the documentary and illustrative material and artefacts used in this research. They almost inevitably went beyond the strict demands of duty in their efforts to be of assistance. I also thank their successors and later day equivalents. Any assistance from the electronic age is frequently more than offset by the weight of the leaden hands of bureaucracy and budgets. Nevertheless they maintain, to the best of their ability, the standards of their predecessors and I am most grateful.

De Havilland Aircraft Co. Fox Moth Utility Aircraft

It was the afternoon of 4 March 1942 in the fishing outport of Musgrave Harbour on the northeast coast of Newfoundland. A little silver and orange biplane had landed on the snow-covered ice and taxied on skis up to a waiting crowd. A woman, obviously in distress, was gently placed in the tiny cabin between the engine and the pilot (an RCAF Group Captain); and the aircraft was turned around, taxied out, and took off. For those familiar with the aircraft it was reassurance. Fox Moth VO-ADE was still on the job!

It might, at first sight, appear something of an anomaly in a book devoted to Canadian WWII military aircraft, to have a section devoted to a foreign civil aircraft. However, VO-ADE definitely qualifies.

The de Havilland DH83 Fox Moth first flew in early 1932 and a total of 98 were produced between then and 1935, many being sold overseas. This was a very respectable production run in the depths of the Depression. The Fox Moth was a highly successful attempt to produce a light transport combining capacity and economy with a reasonable performance on moderate power. This was obtained by using the basic design and some components of the DH82 Tiger Moth trainer plus a 130 hp Gipsy Major engine. With a cabin that could accommodate up to four passengers (albeit with a high degree of intimacy) or an equivalent cargo, it found a ready market in air circus and air taxi operations as well as for general air transport or for the well-off chap who wanted transportation for himself, his luggage, valet and golf clubs for a weekend at a distant golf course. In addition, the Fox Moth won fame in racing and in long-distance and exploratory flying. The Fox Moth's qualities were such that after WWII de Havilland Canada put the Fox Moth back into production as the DH83C. Between 1946 and January 1948 53 of these were produced.

An agreement, signed in 1935 by the United Kingdom, Newfoundland, Canada and the Irish Free State, committed the four countries to cooperation in the establishment of a Trans-Atlantic air service. Newfoundland was primarily concerned with facilities on the western side of the ocean. On a cost-shared basis with Britain, a facility for water-based

This in-flight photo of VO-ADE was very likely taken during its trials by de Havilland before delivery.

In 1929 the British Commonwealth rationalized civil aircraft registration letters. The UK retained G while the five dominions – Australia, Canada, Newfoundland, New Zealand and South Africa – were allotted VH, CF, VO, ZK and ZS respectively. India was given VT, while VP, VQ and VR were reserved for colonies and protectorates. The three aircraft of the Newfoundland Government Air Services were the first to carry the VO registration. After Confederation in 1949 all VO registered aircraft were speedily given CF registrations.

Captain Fraser and an unidentified assistant pause for the cameraman to record the historic first landing at the Newfoundland Airport landing site, known later as Gander. During WWII it would become RCAF Station Gander, an important Ferry Command stopover and home of the convoy escorts and sub-hunters of several Eastern Air Command squadrons.

aircraft was built at Botwood and an enormous airfield was constructed at what was to become Gander. In connection with this enterprise Newfoundland Government Air Services was established in 1934. Its first two aircraft were late-production Fox Moths registered VO-ABC and ADE; in 1936 a Fairchild 71C VO-AFG was acquired. Imperial Airways initially operated the aircraft for the government and provided the crews. One of the first pilots was the Newfoundland pioneer flyer and aviation entrepreneur Douglas Cowan Fraser, who was to do much of the Air Services' total flying time.

For the years before the war the Air Services provided general air transportation for the government including mercy flights, but was primarily involved in establishing the facilities for the trans-Atlantic service, including extensive site surveys and pioneering meteorological flights. On 11 January 1938 VO-ADE made the first landing at Gander. The aircraft were based at Norris Arm on the mouth of the Exploits River, where, in 1935 during an August storm, both Fox Moths were badly damaged at their moorings. VO-ABC had to be written off and its parts used to repair ADE. The Fairchild crashed in 1940, but ADE just kept going, including, besides its other duties, continued survey work on behalf of the Canadians and Americans for their new Newfoundland airfields.

The RCAF had been operating from Newfoundland since June 1940, and a Canada/Newfoundland agreement signed 17 April 1941 transferred the administration and operation of Newfoundland airfields to Canada for the duration of the war. The Newfoundland government jumped the gun when, in late February 1941, Captain Fraser, at Gander, after a search for the crashed Hudson carrying Sir Frederick Banting, the discoverer of insulin, was ordered to turn over ADE to the RCAF and return to St. John's by train. Instead he flew the Fox Moth to St. John's, dismantled it there, and sent it by rail to the Canadians at Gander, complete with a mourning bow in black paint around the cowling.

In justice to the RCAF, for the next three years the Fox Moth performed much the same tasks as before. Indeed, the fact that no other aircraft capable of operating from skis was at Gander in early 1941 may account for the eagerness to acquire VO-ADE. Allotting it an RCAF serial was discussed, but never implemented.

Its fate is somewhat obscure. While it is reported as having crashed at Gander Bay in 1944, it was almost certainly still flying in January 1945. The RCAF did have one instructional Fox Moth airframe A135, which has sometimes been quoted as formerly VO-ADE. However, such an early serial combined with ADE's long life and the general unlikelihood of this transformation makes this identification extremely doubtful.

Above: VO-ADE at Quidi Vidi a short time after being rebuilt to airworthiness using parts from her storm-battered stablemate VO-ABC. Note the modified sliding canopy, larger venturi (nipped tubular fixture to the rear of the cabin windows) and orange-finished tail.

Left: VO-ADE on skis, now an RCAF aircraft, taxis in at Gander in February 1942 after a flight attempting to locate a crashed Hudson of 11 (BR) Squadron.
LAC PA500843

Both the author and the publisher/illustrator have a personal interest in VO-ADE. Carl Vincent's mother was the woman referred to in the first paragraph. As a result of this flight, his younger sister was the first baby born in Gander. Norris Arm, where the Fox Moth was based, is the hometown of Terry Higgins.

De Havilland DH83 Fox Moth #4094, Newfoundland civil registration VO-ADE. Operated by the station flight at RCAF Station Gander from the spring of 1941 until at least early 1945.

all Fox Moth photos (except bottom of p.2) - Stuart Fraser collection

Together with Fox Moth VO-ABC, this aircraft was delivered in a two colour finish comprised of overall aluminum dope with "Imperial Airways orange" upper surfaces. The lower surfaces were further treated with 3 coats of bitumastic paint to preserve the finish during frequent waterborne operations. Compared to other standard production Fox Moths they also featured a vertical tail of larger overall area, probably to offset the adverse yaw effect of the floats. This change is evident in the one extra rib in both the fixed and the rudder portions of the tail plus a slight forward increase in chord of the fixed portion. To further facilitate extended operations from Newfoundland's austere outport and inland operating sites, a dozen or so other more minor changes were introduced at the factory.

Both aircraft entered Newfoundland Government Air Services inventory with wheel, ski, and float undercarriage. The wheels appear to have been factory standard. The skis, supplied by De Havilland Canada, were made up of Elliott Brothers runners on D.H. Canada pedestals. The runners were dark lacquered wood with sheet-metal pedestals and metal fittings. Though a Fairchild Aircraft Ltd. design, the floats were also purchased through De Havilland Canada. They featured orange walkways over lacquered bare metal tops, white marine paint sides and bottoms, and hard rubber nose bumpers.

In August 1935 these aircraft were damaged at their moorings in Norris Arm during a severe storm. VO-ABC was written-off and cannibalized to rebuild VO-ADE to flying status. Post-rebuild VO-ADE featured a slightly heightened sliding cockpit hood with a new reinforcing frame, a larger instrumentation venturi tube on the port side, and a repainted (orange) vertical tail. Additionally, Captain Fraser seems to have devised some sort of heating blanket for the aircraft's oil tank (see inset photo).

While dismantling this aircraft to hand it over to the RCAF Captain Fraser painted a black ribbon (also visible in this photo) around its cowl to mourn its loss to Newfoundland.

Consolidated
Catalina I
Maritime Patrol Aircraft

23 July 1941 – 5:30 pm, a clear day with perfect visibility. Catalina Z2138 of 116 (BR) Squadron, RCAF, two hours out of Dartmouth on a navigation exercise, spotted a fully surfaced submarine with its oblivious crew, who became "most perturbed," and quickly crash-dived. The Catalina dropped two 500 pound (227 kg) anti-submarine bombs, which failed to explode, and the sighting report to EAC was so garbled in transmission as to be unreadable. But it was felt the Catalina had at last seen action.*

While the RCAF's Catalinas have been overshadowed by (and frequently confused with) the Cansos and Canso A's they were a significant addition to its anti-sub force and are an excellent illustration of the tortuous aircraft procurement process the RCAF faced in WWII. Its selection is not surprising – the Consolidated Model 28, known, among other things as PBY, Catalina and Canso, is unquestionably the best known, most numerous and most successful of WWII flying boats. It was employed by every major Allied air service and manufactured in the US, USSR and Canada. Not a new design – it entered USN service in 1936 – its low speed and uninspiring air and waterborne characteristics were more than compensated for by strength, reliability and truly phenomenal endurance. It was the fifth USN model, the PBY-5, upon which the RAF based the version it ordered in January 1940 as the Catalina I.

Canada had shown an early interest in the type. The last-minute RCAF purchasing mission rushed to the US in late August 1939 attempted to purchase 15 but was deterred by the 6 to 12 month delivery time. However, during the winter of 1939-40 the RCAF, faced with the limitations of the Stranraer [see p.38], chose the PBY as its successor. The RCAF had already become disenchanted with flying boats as EAC could only operate them for half the year. Fortuitously, an amphibian version, the PBY-5A, had made its first flight in November 1939. In the spring of 1940 the RCAF had formulated a requirement for 54 of the amphibians – enough for three squadrons, increasing this to six at the escalation of the war in May. The Department of

Munitions and Supply was requested to begin negotiations with Consolidated for 105 amphibians to be assembled in Canada. Eventually, the RCAF agreed, for speed of delivery reasons, that the first 50 could be completed in the US. Later, at the urging of Munitions and Supply, anxious to lock the production line space, the RCAF reluctantly agreed to accept the first 36 of the order as flying boats. Arrangements were made for the last 55 amphibians to be assembled by Boeing Aircraft of Canada in Vancouver, who would also manufacture the tail section, outer wing and floats. Because, in the name of "efficiency" the Canadians had to work through the British Purchasing Mission in the US, the contract was not signed until 5 December 1940. Besides these aircraft, the RCAF was later to order more amphibians from Canadian Vickers while, further on, both Canadian companies built flying boats and amphibians for the Allies.**

The first of the PBY's was not expected until September 1941 and the Battle of the Atlantic was not only intensifying but moving westward as the U-boats tried to outrange the defences. Observing this, the RCAF repeatedly asked both the Americans and British to release PBY's from their contracts, without success. Finally, on 20 May 1941, U-boats sank five ships from Convoy HX126 less than 700 miles from Newfoundland, which galvanized the British Air Ministry into offering the RCAF nine Catalinas awaiting delivery. These were to be returned or replaced when deliveries from the Canadian contract commenced. The RAF Catalinas were picked up in June 1941 and were rushed into RCAF service.

Above: Catalina "D" of 116 (BR) Squadron unleashes a full load of 250lb depth charges from what appears to be a near ideal height circa April 1943. By this time the aircraft featured a radar installation and a repaint while the squadron was using only the single aircraft-in-squadron letter for ID markings. *DND RE64-1044*

Opposite page: Z2138 as ZD • D of 116 (BR) at Dartmouth on 18 September 1941 during a photo op with damage repairs underway after a storm-induced barge collision earlier that day. Interestingly, the RAF-origin serial is carried on the wing undersurfaces in true RCAF early-war style. Although the aircraft has been in service for only about 4 months, the lower hull paintwork is already showing substantial wear and touch-up, some of which are presumably related to the repairs. The illustration on page 6 shows the finish before this incident had taken place. *LAC PL5951*

* This enigmatic episode has never been satisfactorily explained. It was recorded in the unit diary, and a Court of Inquiry held on the subject of the A/S bombs, where the attack was taken at face value. Certainly, during WWII as many air attacks on U-boats were erroneous as were genuine. However, the evidence here seems very clear. Postwar, the only crew member to survive the war wrote to the Chief of Air Staff to enquire about the silence. The CAS referred it to the Air Historian and took no further action. One is compelled to wonder. Certainly, no U-boat was in the vicinity. But, if a submarine was attacked – and it very much appears that one was – whose was it? We will probably never know.

In the meantime, Consolidated was ahead of schedule on the Canadian contract and the first flying boats reached Rockcliffe on 23 August. By now, the RAF was finding itself desperately short of long-range aircraft for Coastal Command and on 7 September asked the RCAF not only to return the nine Catalinas but to give it all fifty of the Canadian aircraft now being delivered. The RCAF response was quite generous. It totally refused to give up the precious amphibians, but agreed to return the RAF Catalinas and give up all 36 of its own flying boats as well as offering to transfer two EAC squadrons to the UK to operate them. The last offer was refused – Coastal Command was short of planes, not men.

It was finally agreed that until the amphibians arrived the RCAF would retain the RAF Catalinas plus the first seven Canadian flying boats delivered. The remaining 29 flying boats were turned over – 11 at Rockcliffe and 18 at the factory. Nine went to the RAAF just in time to be thrown into the Coral Sea and Solomon Islands battles and the remainder to the RAF. All were supposed to be replaced by Catalinas from future RAF contracts. The RCAF's amphibians were delivered in December 1941 and January 1942. However, the face of the war had changed by then, with the Japanese entry into the war and the U-boats moving in on North America. So when, on 11 December 1941, the RAF asked about the nine Catalinas and seven Cansos it was

informed that the deal was off. Canada was going to hang onto them and that was that! The RAF replaced the 29 Canadian aircraft that it received by deducting the nine Catalina I's and giving the RCAF eight Catalina IB's and 12 Catalina IV's in December 1942 and May 1943. At least 17 of these aircraft were assigned to WAC.

During all this time the original Catalinas were hard at work. They were originally issued to EAC's senior flying boat squadron, 5 (BR) at Dartmouth, NS, but, for some reason, within a few days 116 (BR) was reactivated with the Catalinas and some of the 5 (BR) crew, while the disgruntled rump of 5 (BR) soldiered on with the unsatisfactory Stranraers.

The Catalinas flew their first shipping protection operations on 21 June. This was feasible as the RCAF had posted to Dartmouth some pilots who had been on loan to the RAF ferrying the type across the Atlantic. Nonetheless, qualified aircrew and specialists were still in short supply and no auxiliary equipment and spares had been *text continued on page 7*

** *Catalina and Canso: The distinction between the RCAF's Catalinas, Cansos and Canso A's has frequently been a source of confusion. Essentially, the Catalina was initially a version of the Consolidated Model 28 flying boat (USN PBY) ordered for the RAF and built to its specifications. When the RCAF ordered its own Model 28's both US- and Canadian-built, it opted for Canadian versions of the USN PBY-5 and PBY-5A rather than of the RAF's Catalina. There were a number of specifically Canadian features, but the major structural difference was in the wing centre-section. The USN and RAF had entirely different arrangements and locations for supporting the offensive load – apparent in photographs – which were reflected in the internal structure of the wing. The RCAF had a number of changes in nomenclature for these aircraft before they had ever received any. At first they were to be called "Convoy," but it was realized that this would be confusing. Then a number of names of Canadian coastal towns beginning with C were mooted (including Canso, Chimo and Chebucto for the east and Comox, Chinook and Courtenay for the west), with the front runners being Canso for the flying boat and Comox for the amphibian. In February 1941 it was decided to stick with the RAF designation and call them Catalina and Catalina A. When, however, the RCAF was eventually able to compare physically the ex-RAF Catalinas with those built to RCAF specs, it found that the wing centre sections were totally non-interchangeable and the outer wings only after extensive re-wiring. Finally the Air Staff stated that the RCAF aircraft "were, in effect, not Catalinas" and, on 19 December 1941, they were designated Cansos and Canso A's. Some later marks of lend-lease Catalinas had the USN-type centre section, and so were more compatible with Cansos, but those that reached the RCAF were still known as Catalinas.*

The RCAF during WWII took on strength 30 ex-RAF Mk.I, IB and IV Catalina flying boats, seven Canso flying boats (US-built) and 218 Canso A amphibians (14 US-built, 55 Boeing Canada and 149 Canadian Vickers).

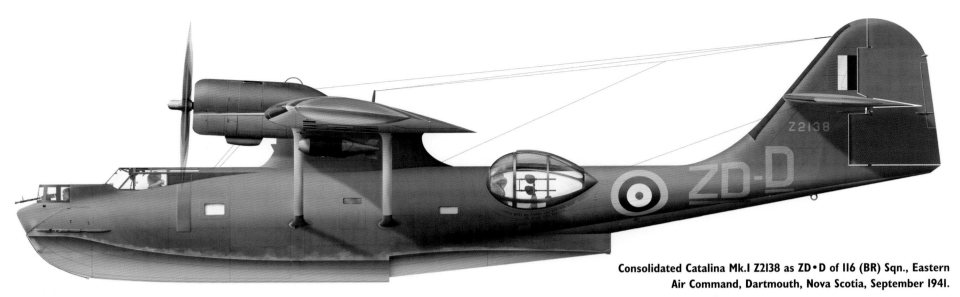

Consolidated Catalina Mk.I Z2138 as ZD•D of 116 (BR) Sqn., Eastern Air Command, Dartmouth, Nova Scotia, September 1941.

Catalina I Z2138 appears to have been finished in the standard early-war RAF scheme for Coastal Command flying boats. This was the Temperate Sea Scheme made up of Dark Slate Grey and Extra Dark Sea Grey on the top and side surfaces with Sky undersurfaces. Interestingly the 10/7/41 amendment to Air Maintenance Order (AMO) A.926/40, the official document detailing the scheme, names the underside colour thus: "The under-surfaces of all aircraft are to be painted duck-egg blue (Sky-Type 'S')" in section 4 covering RAF flying boats, float planes, and amphibians. Standard RCAF markings were applied to Z2138 in the form of large serial numbers repeated under each wing and roundels in 6 positions. The photo on page 5 suggests that the Canadian stock Sky paint was lighter than its initial US factory-applied counterpart, as the repaired areas of the hull have been spot refinished in a lighter shade; it could also be a lighter paint altogether, not necessarily Sky. Presumably the under surface of the wing has also been refinished in a lighter variation. The squadron and aircraft-in-squadron codes take up much of the rear fuselage flanks. The factory-applied serials were usually painted in black somewhere in this area. Those shown here appear to be reapplied in the same colour as the codes, but further back on the tail at the same time that the codes themselves were applied locally. Though concrete evidence has not been obtainable, it would seem likely that early in its service Z2138's rear blister guns were the same as those on RAF Catalina Is — namely twin Vickers VGO .303s. Further, since the RCAF were progressively upgrading such installations with the more capable belt-fed Browning M2 .30cal (see Bolingbroke IV, p.20 and Stranraer, p.38), there is no reason to suppose that Z2138 did not receive the twin Brownings then in use on the Canadian-built Cansos by 1943. All underwing markings were removed by this time as well.

Consolidated Catalina Mk.I Z2138 as aircraft D of 116 (BR) Sqn., Eastern Air Command, Botwood, Newfoundland, April 1943.

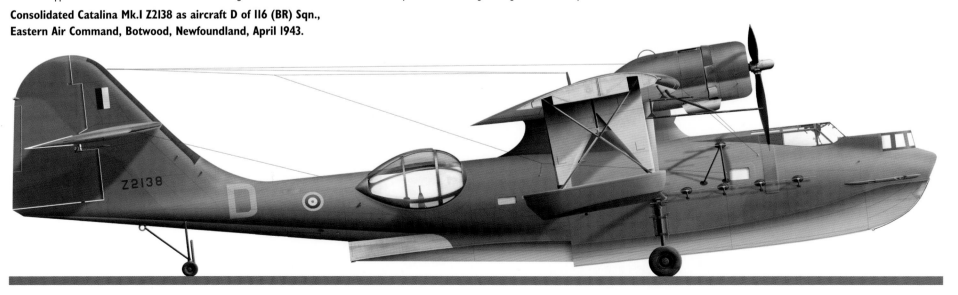

provided. For example beaching gear had to be borrowed from California, Bermuda and Trinidad and in mid-July four aircraft were grounded for lack of fuses, the nearest supply of which was in Chicago! In July a four-plane detachment was stationed at the transatlantic flying boat base in Botwood, Newfoundland, where it conducted operations nearly non-stop. Ice forced the Catalinas out of Botwood on 15 November, before the U-boats really moved close to North America, reinforcing the RCAF's lack of enthusiasm for flying boats. The remaining 116 (BR) Catalinas were kept busy, not only on patrols and convoy escorts, but also picking up spares and equipment from half the hemisphere, surveying long-range ferry routes and transporting surveyors and supplies to Northwest River, Labrador for the new air base at Goose Bay. On one of the latter flights, Z2139 crashed, drowning two crew members. It was later salvaged, used as a pattern aircraft by Canadian Vickers, repaired and rejoined EAC. There were the usual minor incidents – e.g. our subject aircraft Z2138, caught up by the wash of a passing motor torpedo boat, was flung against a barge and suffered damage to its bow. With the onset of winter, the Catalinas having been built to RAF rather than RCAF standards, gave considerable trouble, particularly with cold-weather starting.

For the next two years, supplemented by Cansos, 116 (BR)'s Catalina I's shuttled between Dartmouth, Botwood and Shelburne, Nova Scotia, according to season. The useless anti-sub bombs were replaced by 450-pound (204 kg) depth charges and then by more effective 250-pound (113 kg) ones. They were eventually adorned with the spreading racks of ASV II radar. Sub attacks were few – this was before the U-boats fought it out on the surface – and unlike the nimble Hudsons the ponderous Catalinas could rarely catch one before it submerged. However their constant presence and surveillance was a major asset in securing the Atlantic lifeline. Finally, starting in August 1943, 116 (BR) started to convert to Canso A's and soon after the Catalinas were transferred to the West coast and 3 OTU to finish the war.

Below: Though much smaller than the 450lb Mk.VII used early in the war, the first 250lb depth charge, the Mk.VIII featuring shallow depth detonation and a higher yield explosive, was a much more lethal weapon against surfaced or submerging U-boats. Depending on the aircraft type, the smaller size and lighter weight also gave varying degrees of payload, range and endurance advantage. Along with better detonator pistols and explosives, various air-tails (to improve drop aerodynamics) and several nose shapes (to slow water entry and reduce bounce) were also employed as the basic design evolved towards its ultimate wartime form, the Mk.XI. Under the wing of a banking convoy-protection Canso are what appear to be early Mk.XI's.

Harry Mochulsky Collection via Larry Milberry

Adapted for aircraft use by the British early on and subsequently entering RCAF service in July/August 1941, the 450lb Mk.VII naval depth charge featured aerodynamic nose and tail fairings of several different designs, carriage lug adapter rings, and a new detonator pistol more suitable for the shallow depth operation required of aircraft-borne attacks. The above photo shows a pair with the later-design fairings under a Canso wing, while at left an earlier Canso carries an early Canadian adaptation slung on a British Stores Adaptor as it banks over the torpedoed SS Waterton in Cabot Strait on 11 October 1942. The profile illustration opposite shows a similar round on the Catalina I's Universal Bomb Carrier.

North American Mustang I

Recce Fighter

The North American P-51 Mustang is unarguably among the most important fighters of WWII. However, and with some reason, most attention has been focused on the later models which, with their Rolls Royce Merlin engines, won air superiority over Germany and Japan. The first Mustangs, Allison powered, tend to be glossed over as a prequel before the narrator gets on to the more famous later versions. Nevertheless, in the hands of the RAF and RCAF, these aircraft played a significant part in the air war over Europe from the time they entered service in mid 1942 until nearly the end of the war.

The story of the Mustang, designed in a very short time by North American for the RAF with great attention to aerodynamic detail, is well known. Tested in the UK, it proved to have very pleasant handling characteristics, a long range compared to British fighters and high performance when employed at low and medium altitudes. These qualities resulted in it being issued to Army Cooperation rather than Fighter Command.

The type entered Allied squadron service for the first time in early 1942. Two RCAF squadrons, 400 and 414, received their first in June, replacing the highly unsatisfactory Tomahawks. This rapid re-equipment may have been due to General AGL McNaughton, commanding 1st Canadian Army, who had advanced ideas concerning tactical air power. Indeed, when informed that lack of airfields was delaying the concentration of RCAF army cooperation squadrons into a wing, he assigned the Royal Canadian Engineers to construct an airfield at Dunsfold in Surrey – a task accomplished in six months – the normal British time would be a year! From December 1942 it would be the home of 39 (Army Cooperation) Wing RCAF, which had been formed in September with first 400, then 414 Squadrons and finally, in January 1943, 430 Squadron. All three were Mustang equipped and directly attached to 1st Canadian Army.

text continued on page 10

F/O Frank Hanton and F/O Tony Stephens in Mustangs AL971 SP·S and AG658 SP·T returning from the Dieppe raid, 19 August 1942. Frank Hanton was later to claim 400 Squadron's first aerial victory – a Bf109 on 7 November 1942 – and was to become the squadron's (and probably the Allies') premier "trainbuster."
photo: via Frank Hanton

AL971 in October 1942. This Mustang I went to the RAF as part of the first serial batch of the second British direct purchase contract (contract A-1493 of 17 Sept. 1940) for Mustang aircraft. Seen here less than 6 months after entering squadron service, the airframe is already showing signs of very active service. Note the worn, chipped finish around the filler panel just forward of the windscreen and on the wing root, wing tip, and canopy areas on this side of the aircraft. The progressively modified upper portion of the camouflage scheme is also made evident by the uncharacteristic (for an RAF scheme) patchiness of the colour demarcations. The relatively dark tone of the underside, no doubt combined with the stark high contrast lighting of the photo series presented here, has led some observers to believe erroneously that the undersides were painted black.
photo: Joe Scott

All aircraft of the two initial non-Lend-Lease RAF Mustang orders were delivered through late 1941 — mid 1942 in the early specification RAF camouflage for army cooperation aircraft; the Temperate Land Scheme of Dark Earth and Dark Green upper surfaces with Sky undersides to AMO A.926/40 standard. However the factory colours used were not the actual Ministry of Aircraft Production (MAP) specified shades, but rather near equivalents produced in the USA by various paint manufacturers. Those made by Dupont were apparently used on the initial Mustangs. This manufacturer's Dark Earth appeared more "greyed out" than its British counterpart while the Dark Green was similarly less intense, often tending towards dark olive green. Dupont's Sky Gray bore little resemblance to the odd greenish, greyish blue dubbed "Sky" by MAP. The prop spinner, rear fuselage band, and code letters were painted with the actual Sky colour after the aircraft arrived in the UK.

Even as these aircraft were enroute, RAF Army Cooperation Command (to which the early Mustang squadrons belonged) had officially adopted the new Day Fighter Scheme of Dark Green and Ocean Grey uppers with Medium Sea Grey undersides. While some ACC Mustang I units retained their factory paint in service, others, like 400 Squadron, refinished their aircraft to approximate the new scheme. Here, the Dark Earth areas were overpainted with Mixed Grey (a darker grey substitute for the new and temporarily unavailable Ocean Grey), the Dark Green areas were left untouched, and the undersides were refinished in Medium Sea Grey. Early on, the US factory applied Type A roundels were overpainted entirely and moved further forward on the fuselage. Later, the fin flashes and fuselage roundels had their white area reduced with the result that they appeared to be slightly disproportioned Type C markings. By the time of the Dieppe operation (August 19, 1942) AL971 was aircraft S of 400 Squadron. It featured several touch-up areas within the upper camouflage colours. The chord-wise Yellow ID bands (as below) appear to have been toned down with Dull Red (as above). The significance of the "SNARD II" inscriptions below the windscreen quarter-lights is not known.

Despite the acquisition of the more potent Mustangs, the squadrons of Army Cooperation Command had, of necessity, to spend much of their time in training with the army in preparation for the time it would go back to war. This, plus familiarization with their new mounts, occupied the two RCAF squadrons until 19 August 1942, when they took their Mustangs into action for the first time, in support of the disastrous Dieppe landing. Their task, along with two RAF Mustang squadrons, was to provide tactical reconnaissance on an hourly or half-hourly basis over all the inland approaches to report on German reinforcements – 72 Mustang sorties in all. While no reinforcements had been dispatched, the Mustangs were at constant risk from fighters and the alerted light flak. This cost a total of 9 Mustangs – including one each from the RCAF units. As some recompense, the first Mustang kill, an FW190, was made by F/O HH Hills of 414.

Following Dieppe, the RCAF Mustang units, besides interminable training, flew *Populars* – low altitude photo recce sorties over enemy territory and, starting in the fall of 1942, *Rhubarbs*. These were daylight offensive sorties, normally flown in bad weather, against specific targets – mainly airfields and aircraft as well as all forms of transportation, but railway locomotives in particular. By mid-1943 400 and 414, with 430 not far behind, were well into their stride. In April 1943, 400 Squadron broadened its operational spectrum by adding night

Ranger sorties, scoring its first night aerial victory on 15 August. Space prohibits detailing the RCAF Mustang units' successes. Let it be said, though, that they were far and away the leading train-busters of 83 Group – 400 Squadron destroyed or badly damaged over 100 locomotives in six months while 400 and 414 between them scored the greater percentage of all RAF/RCAF Mustang I victories. These successes were not without losses, most inflicted by the enemy's highly effective light flak and the hazards of low-level operations at all hours and in all weather.

In late 1943, 400's duties were changed to high altitude PR and in January and February 1944 the Mustangs gave way to Mosquito PR XVI's and Spitfire PR XI's. 414 continued with Mustangs to the Normandy landings and beyond till attrition forced conversion to Spitfire IX's in August 1944 [see p.46] while 430 operated its venerable Mustangs until December 1944.

More photos of AL971 taken at the same time as that on the bottom of p.8. These appear to have been misinterpreted elsewhere as showing an experimental night operational camouflage including black undersurfaces. A close examination of the entire series of original prints indicates that this was not the case. In the high-contrast lighting provided by the open sky the highlights appear "blown out" while the shadows are "blocked up". Yet portions of the underside Medium Sea Grey are still quite visible, especially at the wing root and tip. *photos: LAC PA138760, PA138768*

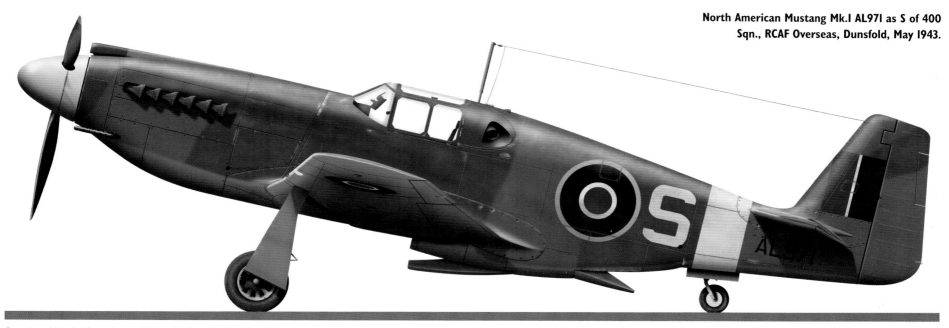

Sometime within the 10 months after Dieppe, AL971 received new flame-damping exhausts and an oblique reconnaissance camera behind the pilot's headrest, physical testament to the Mustang I's evolving tactical roles of hunter by night and armed observer by day. There is also evidence that the paint job has been revised to full RAF Day Fighter spec. (compare to that on p.9). The chordwise ID stripes are now absent, the serial has been reapplied further back on the fuselage in "proper" RAF-style characters and the "Snard II" inscription appears to have been overpainted. Several methods of re-paneling the quarterlight over the new camera installation are in evidence on both U.S. and Commonwealth service tactical reconnaissance Mustang I's. In the photo below AG528 B features a modified clear Perspex panel while AL971 S has a painted panel in place of its clear original. Each aircraft also features differently shaped cut-outs for the camera lens' line-of-sight. Although only a few of these external differences are evident in photographs, mission-specific configurations and progressive camera installation upgrades led to a surprisingly large variety of detail changes, mostly internal, in this area. The new Kittyhawk-type exhausts were preferred by the RAF over their US counterparts as they were less prone to overheating and cracking. The radiator intake and exhaust flaps are in the fully opened position and the elevator is in nose-down trim, typical of a Mustang I at rest.

400 Squadron Mustangs on a typical three-aircraft concrete hardstand at Dunsfold in June 1943. Our illustration subject, AL971 S, is on the right. Squadron codes had been eliminated from Mustangs by this time, leaving only the single aircraft-in-squadron letter. The new flame-damping exhausts were especially beneficial during night Ranger missions which had commenced a month earlier. Light reflecting off the relatively light coloured concrete illuminates the underside finish and details quite well. Although the squadron went on to become a dedicated photo-reconnaissance unit with unarmed Spitfires and Mosquitoes at the end of the year, some of the venerable Mustangs were retained through the early months of 1944. The other two squadrons in 39 Wing continued in the tactical fighter recce role [see p.46]. *photo: LAC PA146138*

Fleet **Fort** Wireless Trainer

The Fleet Fort, the only Canadian–designed trainer to achieve production in WWII, long remained an unpublicized enigma. After prototype publicity, very little was written about its wartime service. Only after a third of a century did it become the subject for historical research and its highly fraught career described.*

The Fort represented Fleet's attempt to consolidate its previous success in the trainer field by producing an all-metal monoplane advanced trainer. The Fleet 60 (designated the 60K Fort in its production version) was conceived in 1938 and, among other modern features had separate enclosed cockpits, with the instructor behind and above the pupil, and a fixed undercarriage with ingenious semi-retractable wheel fairings (later abandoned). In production it was powered by a 330 hp Jacobs radial engine.

The prototype did not fly until early 1940. It was evaluated by the RCAF in May and a contract placed in June for 200 for use as an intermediate trainer. Tooling for the assembly line was very slow and the first production aircraft was not completed until May 1941. The first nine Forts were used for testing or issued to 2 SFTS for trial use in its designed role. These were plagued by mechanical difficulties and were rarely serviceable. These faults, plus the fact that the role of intermediate trainer was now seen as redundant, led to the reduction of the Fort order to 100 (RCAF serials 3561 to 1660 – plus prototype 3540). The last Fort was delivered in June 1942.

The Forts were now to serve as wireless trainers. They were converted, not by Fleet, but by RCAF repair depots, by fitting an R1082/T1083 radio set in place of the rear instrument panel, a DF loop and an aerial mast as part of the turnover pylon. They then saw service in the two western BCATP wireless schools – 2 WS, Calgary and 3 WS, Winnipeg, for two years from the spring of 1942. They saw non-stop service and were instrumental in turning out a large percentage of the Plan's production of wireless operators for this period. However, in 2 WS especially, their poor flying and landing traits, propensity for undercarriage failures and mid-air fires, and general unserviceability made them greatly disliked. Indeed, they seem to have precipitated a near-mutiny by the 2 WS staff pilots. To be fair, 3 WS, which operated fewer Forts seems to have had less trouble, but still suffered its share of crashes. Indeed, at least a quarter of the WS Forts met violent ends.

In justice to Fleet, the Fort with its metal construction was very different from the aircraft types it had previously built and this, combined with the rapid wartime expansion of its facilities and work force, was partly responsible for the Fort's problems.

After their replacement by Yales and Harvards, the Forts saw no further service. Now only the two lovingly restored [one to flying status – Ed.] examples owned by the Canadian Warplane Heritage remain to commemorate one of Canada's more interesting, even if less successful, aircraft.

* For the full story see: "Fleet's Indefensible Fort" by Dave Fletcher and Carl Vincent, High Flight, Vol. 1, No. 2 (1981).

Right: Forts of 2 WS, Calgary. This photo of 3610 and 3609 (subject of our profile) shows the typical tail-heavy flying attitude of the wireless-equipped Fort.

Below: a nice 3/4 rear view of Fort 3609, our subject aircraft.

Fleet Fort 3609, No.2 Wireless School, Calgary, Alberta, circa 1942 - 1943.

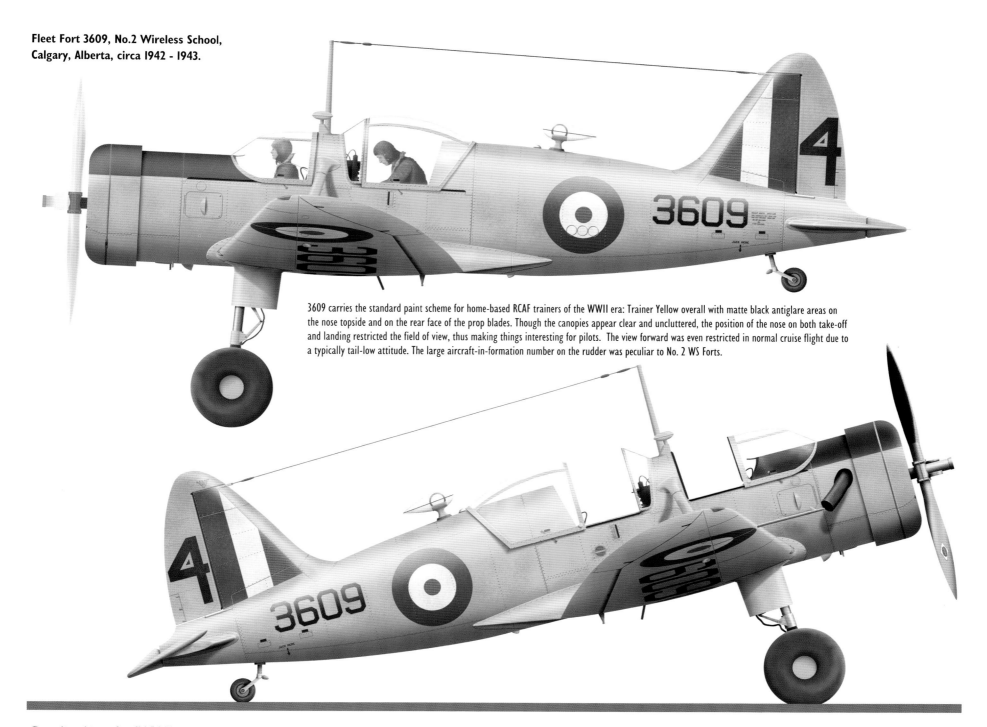

3609 carries the standard paint scheme for home-based RCAF trainers of the WWII era: Trainer Yellow overall with matte black antiglare areas on the nose topside and on the rear face of the prop blades. Though the canopies appear clear and uncluttered, the position of the nose on both take-off and landing restricted the field of view, thus making things interesting for pilots. The view forward was even restricted in normal cruise flight due to a typically tail-low attitude. The large aircraft-in-formation number on the rudder was peculiar to No. 2 WS Forts.

Short Sunderland III
Maritime Patrol Aircraft

Of all the large aircraft types that served with RAF Coastal Command during WWII, the one that will probably come to mind most readily is the Short Sunderland. While it possessed neither the endurance of the Catalina nor the range and speed of the Liberator, the ruggedness, capacity, seaworthiness and defensive capability of this massive machine made it immensely popular with its crews. It served from the first day of the war to the last, when there were no less than 28 Sunderland squadrons – two of them RCAF. Coincidentally, 28 submarines were destroyed by Sunderlands, six by the Canadian squadrons.

The Sunderland was designed to meet a specification for a four-engined monoplane flying boat to replace the biplanes that had equipped RAF squadrons to date. Short Brothers,

probably Britain's premier designers of marine aircraft, successfully submitted a design that drew heavily on the experience gained with the S-23 C-class Empire boats. The prototype Sunderland flew in October 1937, by which time a contract for 21 had already been placed. Powered by four Bristol Pegasus XXII's and with a defensive armament that included two power-operated turrets the type was an immediate success. By the start of the war it equipped four RAF squadrons. 75 Sunderland I's and 58 II's were built by Short Brothers in Belfast and later by Blackburn in Dumbarton, Scotland before the definitive version, the Sunderland III went into production by both firms in 1942. It was around this time that the RCAF came into the picture.

In the spring of 1942 the RAF hastily transferred three Catalina squadrons, including 413 Squadron RCAF, to the Far East, which left only six flying boat squadrons in the UK. Hence, Coastal Command was authorized to form three new squadrons and re-equip a fourth. Two of the new units were supplied by the RCAF – 422 and 423 squadrons. These, the fifth and sixth RCAF units in Coastal Command

were nominally formed in April and May 1942. Both took some time to become operational. 423, initially stationed in Oban, Scotland, did not receive its first Sunderlands until 17 July. Having worked up on these aircraft it was declared operational in October and almost immediately after was moved to Castle Archdale on Lough Erne, inland in County Fermanagh, Northern Ireland, where it was to spend the war. 422's gestation period was more prolonged and difficult. Formed at Lough Erne, its first airman did not arrive until June and, though intended to be a Catalina squadron its first aircraft, seven Saro Lerwicks – possibly the greatest failure of the British aviation industry in WWII – did not appear until late June. Three Catalinas did arrive in early August, but later that month were detached, along with the three most experienced crews, to the Shetlands to cover convoys to Russia. On their return a month later, 422 was ordered to turn over the Cats to an OTU and turn in the Lerwicks for overdue scrapping. The aircraftless squadron aircrew were employed on ferry duties. In November 422 exchanged bases with 423 at Oban and finally started to train

Sub killer EK591 2•U executes a textbook landing at Castle Archdale on July 15th, 1944. The FN11 nose turret appears to have been replaced by a fairing, possibly due to upgrade work in progress. The other turret guns have either been stowed as part of the landing drill, or this was some sort of test hop *sans* guns. Depending on the landing weight, as the power is backed off and the wing loses lift, up to 3 or 4 ft (1-1.2 m) of hull will be below the waterline. It was a very large machine.

photo: LAC PL40996

Short Brothers (Blackburn built) Sunderland Mk.III EK591 as 2•U of 422 Sqn., RCAF Overseas, Castle Archdale, circa early to mid 1944.

EK591

U○2

2○U

Sunderland Mk.III EK591 was finished in the late-war standard Coastal scheme of Extra Dark Sea Grey upper surfaces with the balance of the exterior in White. The MAP specification of 1943 (amended in '44) called for the white portion on Coastal Command flying boats to be matte finish on all surfaces except the wing and tailplane undersurfaces which were to be made glossy by the application of a final coat of transparent covering dope (Stores Ref. 33B/85, 86 or 87). The squadron 2 and individual aircraft U codes are painted Light Slate Grey while the EK591 serial number is black. When Coastal squadrons went to this single numeral code format [see also p.48 Beaufighter], instead of right-reading on both sides of the fuselage, 422's application could be unique in sometimes having the aircraft letter to the rear and squadron numeral ahead of the roundel on both sides, or sometimes opposite to spec on both sides, and rarely to spec.

The waterline weathering, weather-beaten de-icer boot coating (wing and tail leading edges), vertical grime streaking adjacent to the wings, and horizontal stains on the engine cowls are typical of operational Sunderlands. As the first Mk.I's and Mk.II's entered service the standard ASW weapons were the 250lb and 500lb A/S bombs. The more effective 450lb Mk.VII depth charge quickly supplanted these nearly useless weapons. By the time that most front line squadrons were flying Mk.III's and IIIA's, 8x 250lb d/cs was the standard long-range load. Depending on mission range/endurance requirements, sometimes more could be carried in the aircraft's cavernous hold so that the wing racks could be reloaded in flight via built-in ordnance handling gear! *photo: LAC PL40991*

on Sunderlands, despite the RCAF's protests. Catalinas were preferred. The new aircraft type and the posting out of many crews meant extensive retraining but 422 became operational at last on 1 March 1943.

Bowmore, on Islay in the Inner Hebrides was 422's first operational station. It was a rugged and primitive location – no slipway, so the Sunderlands had to be maintained elsewhere. The squadron stayed there almost six months in uncomfortable circumstances, but getting into the routine of patrols, escorts and sub hunts, all in frequently bad weather. The Battle of the Atlantic had reached its peak and Coastal Command had developed into a formidable anti-sub force. With experience, good operational and electronic intelligence, better aircraft and tactics, plus much improved radar and offensive weaponry the rate of U-boat sinkings had started to rise. The Sunderland had developed right along and now sported radar, a load of 250-pound (113 kg) shallow-set depth charges and a gun armament that included, besides the nose, tail and mid-upper turrets, four fixed guns in the nose and a .5 machine gun at each of the galley hatches.

In May 1943, soon after 422 became operational, the U-boats had a resounding defeat in the North Atlantic and had been temporarily withdrawn from there while new tactics were developed. It saw no action that summer but sustained losses were through flying and landing accidents. In early November it gratefully moved from Bowmore and joined 423 at Castle Archdale, though most of the squadron's accommodation was seven miles (11.25 km) away at St. Angelo.

Just before the move the squadron saw its first action. In September the U-boats had returned, now equipped with a formidable AA armament of 37 and 20 mm guns and orders to travel in groups of two or more and to fight it out on the surface if surprised by an aircraft. The Sunderlands would need all their massive strength and enhanced firepower now – the latter more impressive in volume than impact due to the .303 calibre of most of the guns. On 17 October 1943 Sunderland JM712 J, captained by F/L PT Sargent, homed on a radar contact to two surfaced U-boats, U-448 and U-281, went in through fierce flak without serious damage, but one depth charge hung up and three others undershot. With only two left, Sargent attacked again without taking evasive action. The two depth charges straddled U-448, but both U-boats' guns hit the Sunderland hard, causing severe damage, killing the Group Gunnery Officer who had

manned one of the .5 galley guns and mortally wounding the navigator who was able to plot a course to a convoy before he died. Sargent, badly wounded, ditched near the convoy, but was trapped in the wreckage when the Sunderland sank. U-448 was seriously damaged and had to abort the patrol. 422 Squadron suffered another loss on 20 November when Sunderland W6031 G, was lost with all its crew in an attack on U-648.

The first unalloyed success by a 422 Sunderland featured our subject aircraft EK591 2•U. At 11:25 on 10 March 1944 it took off from Castle Archdale to patrol in an area west of Ireland where a U-boat concentration had been reported. Its crew had recently joined 422 from OTU and the captain, W/O WF Morton was being screened by F/L SW Butler, who was at the controls when U-625 was sighted, 6 miles (9.65 km) to port. Butler took 2•U down to 400 feet (122 m) and both sub and aircraft manoeuvred violently, the former to keep its stern to the aircraft, where the flak could be most effective and the aircraft to get on the bow for the same reason. After 10 minutes Butler settled for a beam attack and, in a steep diving turn, took the Sunderland down to 50 feet (15 m) and corkscrewing through fierce flak, dropped six 250 lb Mk XI Torpex-filled depth charges. Only four were seen to explode – one to starboard and three to port – a straddle almost in line with the conning tower. U-625 submerged but surfaced after three minutes, slowly circling. The Sunderland, having expended its depth charges also circled, signaling for assistance. Eighty minutes later, U-625 flashed a signal *Fine Bombish* and the crew abandoned ship, getting into one large and several small dinghies. The submarine sank at 17:40.

2•U had been hit by a shell in the bow below the waterline during the run-in and as soon as a 423 Squadron Sunderland arrived headed for home. The main shell-hole was patched without difficulty, but numerous smaller holes due to sprung rivets posed more of a problem. The solution was chewing gum. Each crew member had 5 sticks of Wrigley's Spearmint as part of their flight ration and this, suitably

masticated, applied to the leaks and hardened in the cold air did the job. The Sunderland landed safely, and the crew members, besides other recognition, each received a 24-pack of gum from Wrigley's!

U-625's survivors were kept under surveillance by the 423 Sunderland until it had to head for home with no rescue vessels in the vicinity. The U-boat men were never seen again – the North Atlantic in March can be merciless.

This was destined to be 422 Squadron's only success, though 423 had racked up a total of five by November 1944. 422 continued its essential work from Castle Archdale and later from Pembroke Dock, and finished the war in the process of converting to Sunderland V's.

The crew of U-625 abandon ship. The disappearance of these brave men is one of the numerous unobserved tragedies of the Battle of the Atlantic.

photos: Frank Cauley

As seen in the previous pages' photos, turret guns are typically stowed prior to landing. As the aircraft approaches its buoy, the nose turret is retracted and the bollards affixed to facilitate mooring procedures. The turret and its fairing often remain retracted during beaching operations but can be frequently seen fully or partially in the forward position during maintenance and ramp time. The elevators, bomb doors, nose entry door and galley hatch are in typical mooring / beaching positions. The beaching gear is thought to have been finished in aluminum lacquer with red stripes. In the photo below 422 Squadron Sunderlands Mk.IIIA ML883 V and Mk.III ML857 are seen on the Castle Archdale ramp, late June, 1944. Coming from the same Blackburn (Dumbarton) production line as, but built later than, our subject aircraft they illustrate several important aspects of the big flying boat's design evolution. The later ML883 features a twin Browning .303 nose turret, the 4 fixed forward firing guns, the ASV Mk.IVc centimetric radar (the domes under the outer wings) and, very likely though not seen, the .50 calibre Browning mounts in the galley hatches (square openings just behind the beaching gear struts). The earlier ML857 has the old single Vickers .303 nose turret, the less effective ASV Mk.II radar (antenna arrays along the spine, rear fuselage sides, above the cockpit and under the outer wings), and no fixed nose guns. It would appear that sometime between the completion of these two examples, the Sunderland line at Dumbarton switched from Mk.III to Mk.IIIA production. Like the early-build Mk.III EK591, ML857 may receive armament upgrades as the operational schedule permits. It is not known if the galley gun installation was done at the squadron or at maintenance depot level. Note the Catalina, a type which 422 Squadron used to operate, parked behind the third Sunderland in the background.   *photo: PL40985*

Hawker
Hurricane XII Fighter

Saturday morning, 5 September 1942, an hour before noon and a flat calm under a low cloud ceiling in the Wabana anchorage, the sheltered stretch of water between Bell Island and the shore of Conception Bay, Newfoundland. Four ships were either anchored or at the Wabana pier loading or waiting to load iron ore from the mines that ran out under the bay. Suddenly the air was rent by explosions – torpedoes and then gunfire from the ships and from the Newfoundland gunners manning the shore battery. When the sound and spray had subsided two ships had gone to the bottom, 29 merchant seamen had died and U-513 had escaped. Nor was this the end – on 2 November U-518 made a night attack in light rain evading the enhanced defences and sinking two more ships, while another 40 men died.

Not only had the U-boats been able to penetrate ten miles (16.1 km) into the bay, but they had made their kills not much more than a minute's flying time from the RCAF base at Torbay. A 145 (BR) Hudson [see p.59] had made it down through the hills between the 200 foot (61 m) cloud cover and the water on 5 September, but far too late. One measure to improve the anti-sub air defence occurred to the RCAF – a quick-response force using that most versatile of Allied WWII fighters – the Hawker Hurricane.

The basic history of the Hurricane is well-known. It was the mainstay of RAF Fighter Command for the first years of WWII and served overseas even longer and was used in many roles. The RCAF made acquaintance with the type very early. Canada ordered 24 Hurricanes in 1938 and 20 had been delivered by the start of the war, serving with 1 (F) Squadron. This unit was rushed overseas at the end of May 1940, taking the Hurricanes with it and leaving the RCAF with no fighter aircraft for nearly a year and a half (with the exception of the pathetic Grumman Goblin and the unsuitable Bolingbroke). Admittedly air defence was not a major Canadian priority, but German long-range or ship-board aircraft were a distinct possibility while Japanese intentions had become increasingly menacing. Probably, as well, senior Canadian politicians and airmen quaked at the thought of the public reaction to even

Jack Bolye Collection via Larry Milberry

a minor Axis air incursion. Fighter aircraft existed in quantity in Canada at the time – Canadian Car and Foundry in Fort William, Ontario had been producing Hurricanes for the RAF since 1940, but these were totally out of bounds to the RCAF. Indeed Lord Beaverbrook described any such allotment as "a crime against the Empire." Eventually, after much wheeling and dealing, in late 1941 eighty were diverted from British orders while Minister of Munitions CD Howe placed a strictly Canadian order for 400 – a number so far in excess of possible RCAF requirements that 150 were eventually transferred to the RAF.

The final tally of Canadian-built Hurricanes acquired by the RCAF was 30 Mk XI's (Mk.I's with Packard Merlins and RCAF equipment) 400 Mk XII's (Mk.IIB's with Packard Merlins) and 50 Mk XIIA's built as Sea Hurricanes and identical to the XII but with 8-gun armament. By late 1942 there were two Hurricane squadrons in Western and six in Eastern Air Commands. The resident fighter squadron at Torbay was 125 (F) which, on 20 April 1942, had become the first RCAF Hurricane squadron to be formed after the start of the war. Initially equipped with Hurricane XI's, it moved from Sydney, NS, to Torbay on 9 June. The Mk XI's could not easily be fitted with bomb carriers, but were replaced by Mk XII's in November. The prototype bomb carrier installation was completed in January 1943 and tested with both 250 pound (113 kg) depth charges and anti-sub bombs, and 125 (F)'s pilots were astounded to learn of their additional duty. The squadron

CO, S/L RW Norris, explained, "It is our duty to show that a fighter squadron can be used for more than one thing and thus make our position much more interesting while we are waiting to protect our shores from enemy aerial activity. It is our duty to show the BR squadrons that we are as good as they are, and that our skill and knowledge are as good as theirs." For the next six months, until 29 June 1943, 125 (F) flew patrols or maintained Hurricanes on standby, armed with depth charges. By this time, though, the U-boats no longer operated within their range and no contact was made. On 25 June 1943, the squadron returned to Sydney where in late 1943 it was selected as one of three EAC Hurricane squadrons to go overseas. There, renumbered 441 Squadron and flying Spitfires, it compiled a distinguished record in much closer contact with the enemy than when it had toted depth charges over the grey North Atlantic.

Hawker (Canada Car & Foundry built) Hurricane Mk.XII 5495 as aircraft S of 125 (F) Sqn., Eastern Air Command, Torbay, Newfoundland, January to June 1943.

Though built under a specifically RCAF contract, Hurricane XII 5495 featured wing roundels positioned more like those on RAF-destined aircraft (i.e. not extremely close to the wing tips). It wears the typical RAF-standard early war day fighter scheme of Dark Earth and Dark Green with Sky Grey undersides. By the time 125(F) was operational with these unique Eastern Air Command underwing warloads, a well worn finish was typical — especially so around the wing-walk and gun servicing areas. The serial repeated on the cowl side and aircraft-in-squadron letter repeated under the nose were usual during this period for 125(F)s Hurricanes, although the latter is not seen on the trials aircraft in the top photo on page 18. From this photo, as well as from others used as references, it can be seen that gunnery training was a standard practice of the period, as the leading-edge span-wise stripes show signs of repeated doped fabric applications. Such patches were used to cover the gun ports prior to missions on many WWII fighter aircraft. Although the aircraft's manual shows cone-shaped muzzle flash hiders on the 2 outboard guns in each wing of operational day fighters, these do not appear to have been installed on the Torbay Hurricanes.

The locally-developed ordnance carriage system installed for the Torbay quick-reaction ASW mission was a rather crude affair aerodynamically, especially when compared to the neatly faired-over devices then being used by the RAFs fighter-bomber Hurricanes overseas. It comprised a standard Mk.III Universal Bomb Carrier attached directly to the wing hardpoint, suitably sway braced, and what appears to be a simple spacer block to give the load a nose down flight attitude. Note that the depth charges (above) are of the early concave-nosed 250lb Mk.VIII variety, likely surplus to the needs of the "real" ASW units based at Torbay. The even more outmoded 250lb A/S bomb (below) is easily identified in silhouette by its water-entry nose cap.

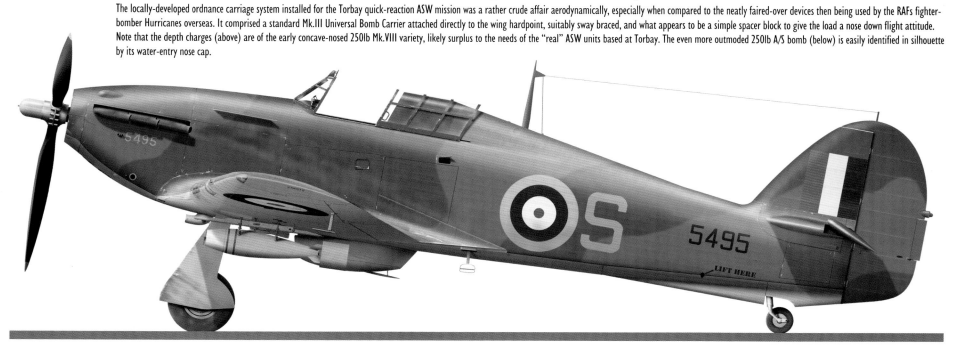

Bristol **Bolingbroke** IV
General Reconnaissance Aircraft

March 23 1942 – a miserable foggy day northeast of Sable Island. The third wave of *Paukenschlag* (Drumbeat) was about to break on the American coast and one of its last subs, U-754, was passing through, tracking stragglers from convoy HX181. It had sunk one, the tanker *British Prudence* and was trying for a second, the elderly American freighter *Bayou Chico*. In an unpublicized episode of the Battle of the Atlantic, the *Bayou Chico* kept the U-boat from getting into attacking position, dodging in and out of the fog and keeping U-754 under continual fire from its deck gun, meanwhile screaming for help. The merchantman eventually escaped in the fog, but its SOS had alerted Bolingbroke 9066 DM·T from 119 (BR)'s Sydney detachment which surprised U-754 on the surface. The pilot, Sgt. CS Buchanan made two separate attacks dropping a single depth charge each time – the tactic of dropping a stick of d/c's had not yet become standard in EAC. The submarine's bow was blown high out of the water each time, and the boat then sank, leaving a trail of bubbles and an oil slick. This action was subsequently publicized as a kill, but while U-754's log, in describing this attack by "a three-engined bomber," recorded that the d/c's were "well placed" the U-boat only suffered minor damage.* However, the Bolingbroke had finally seen action – and in its designated role!

The Bristol Bolingbroke was the first warplane to be built in really significant numbers for the RCAF, serving from the North Atlantic to Bering Strait, as well as becoming a mainstay of the BCATP. However, much of what has been written about it to date has oversimplified its convoluted history to the point of making it incomplete or inaccurate. The following is a very condensed summary of its story [the author is currently working on a complete type history for Aviaeology]. Frequently described as "a Canadian version of the Blenheim IV" the opposite is true. The Bolingbroke was a general reconnaissance aircraft based on the Blenheim I bomber and designed for RAF Coastal Command to bridge the gap between the Anson and the Beaufort. It differed from the Blenheim not only in having a four instead of three-man crew and a dinghy plus other equipment for its maritime role but also an extended nose to improve its poor visibility. Canada first expressed an interest in this aircraft in November 1936, with a view to acquiring 18. The prototype Bolingbroke did not fly until September 1937, by which time the RAF had ordered 139 and the RAAF 40. Canada now was taking steps to greatly expand its aviation industry, so, with some difficulty, Fairchild Aircraft Ltd. obtained a license to build the Bolingbroke upon which the RCAF placed an order for 18. Bolingbroke development was slow – visibility and vibration problems meant that three nose designs had to be prepared while Bristol's focus was concentrated on Blenheim I production and Beaufort design. As a result, in late December 1937 the Air Ministry abandoned plans for Bolingbroke production, leaving Coastal Command to purchase an American type, the

* U-754's escape from destruction at the hands of Eastern Air Command was merely a stay of execution. On 31 July 1942 she was caught on the surface south of Yarmouth, NS, by a Hudson of 113 (BR) Squadron, flown by S/L NE "Mollie" Small – one of EAC's greatest leaders and tacticians. A perfect salvo of four 250-lb d/c's sent U-754 and her crew permanently to the bottom.

Lockheed Hudson, in June 1938, while the extremely angry Australians were left with nothing. Canada, in an uncharacteristic display of firmness, resisted all blandishments to "wait for the Beaufort" and persuaded a reluctant Air Ministry and an even more reluctant Bristol to continue with development of the Bolingbroke airframe, while Fairchild prepared for production based on drawings of those parts that were already definitive.

text continued on p.22

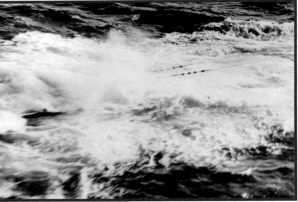

Top: U-754's bow breaks the surface during the attack by Bolingbroke 9066 on 23 March 1942.

Right: Bolingbroke IV 9066, erstwhile hero of the Battle of the Atlantic, on the line with its new stablemates in Western Air Command's 147 (BR) Squadron. Note the mix of Night (black) and Sky underside colours.

photo: LAC SIG270

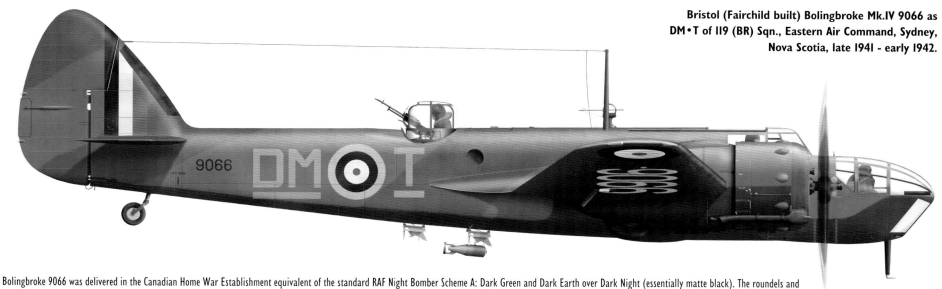

Bristol (Fairchild built) Bolingbroke Mk.IV 9066 as
DM•T of 119 (BR) Sqn., Eastern Air Command, Sydney,
Nova Scotia, late 1941 - early 1942.

Bolingbroke 9066 was delivered in the Canadian Home War Establishment equivalent of the standard RAF Night Bomber Scheme A: Dark Green and Dark Earth over Dark Night (essentially matte black). The roundels and tail flashes are also analogous to their RAF counterparts, though the wing roundels are much further outboard. Code letters are Light Grey with the 2 letter squadron designator and the single letter aircraft-in-squadron designator right-reading on both sides. The White underwing serials read properly inboard from the wingtip on both sides (see below for other side). Being a relatively early-production Mk.IV, 9066 initially carried a Vickers drum-fed VGO gun in its Bristol B.I Mk.II turret. The Light Series Stores Carriers below the fuselage were typically loaded with sea markers (above), practice bombs, or combinations thereof (below). The round window just ahead of the turret station, section of metal skin between the nose and cockpit Perspex to starboard, enlarged fairing for the modified oil system above the starboard engine nacelle, elongated (for dinghy housing) port nacelle, DF loop antenna "football", cabin heat intensifier pipes coming off the rear of the exhaust pipes, de-icer boots on all tail and wing leading edges, and relocated (to-starboard) trailing aerial fairlead are all external features that set the Canadian-built Bolingbroke IV apart from their somewhat outwardly similar British-built Blenheim IV cousins.

**Bristol (Fairchild built) Bolingbroke Mk.IV 9066 as SZ•K of 147 (BR) Sqn.,
Western Air Command, Sea Island, British Columbia, July 11, 1942.**

After reassignment to 147 (BR) Bolingbroke 9066 was re-coded as SZ•K, the previous identity being painted out with what appears to be fresh Dark Earth. Scrutinizing the original photographs, one can just discern the earlier DM•T codes under the new paint. Interestingly, the 119 badge, which contemporary photos of other 119 Bolingbrokes indicate was most probably on the aircraft at the time of its 23 March 1942 action, as well as the U-boat attack marking itself, were left untouched by its new operators (at least up to July 11). By this time the turret had been upgraded to B.I Mk.IVA standard with twin belt-fed Browning .303s in place of the obsolete VGO.

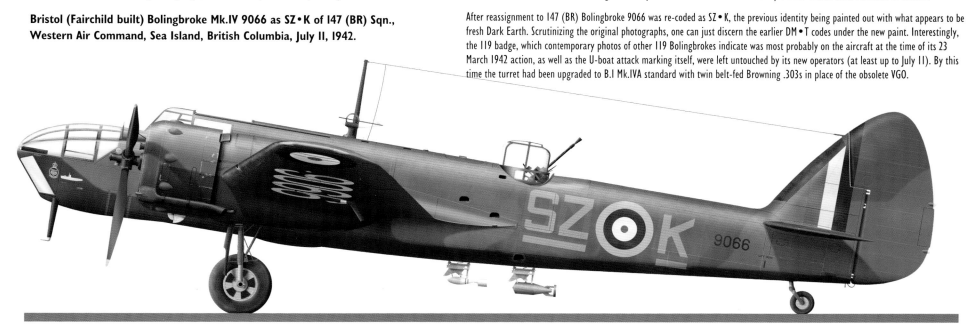

Canadian production was slow to get under way. Delivery of drawings was dilatory and the final version of the Bristol prototype with the production nose did not fly until June 1938. Also, while most of the airframe structure was made in Canada, a host of minor proprietary fittings had to be obtained in the UK. The main spar castings came from Bristol themselves. Half of these proved to be under minimum strength and required reworking. These delays plus those inherent in producing a complicated aircraft for the first time meant that the first Mk.I Bolingbroke did not fly until September 1939.** Meanwhile the RAF, impressed by the Bolingbroke's qualities, had upgraded the Blenheim I bomber by fitting the Bolingbroke nose and, later, wing fuel tanks and Mercury XV engines instead of Mercury VIII's. As a bomber rather than a GR type it was designated a Blenheim – the Mk.IV. It took the Mk.I's place on the production line and thus entered service well before the

Bolingbroke – hence the oft-parroted myth that the latter was the Canadian version of the Blenheim IV. In addition to the GR features of the British Bolingbroke, the RCAF's Mk.I's featured cabin and carburetor heating, wing, tail and airscrew de-icing, a pressure fire extinguisher and fittings to permit its conversion to a seaplane.

The first RCAF Bolingbroke squadron was intended to be 8 (BR) which was flying Northrop Deltas from North Sydney and Sydney, Nova Scotia [see p.29]. From November 1939, detachments of air and ground crew were posted to Rockcliffe for training on the first few Bolingbrokes off the line. Although training was severely handicapped by serviceability problems, by the spring all aircraft produced had crews. The 8 (BR) Bolingbroke detachment moved to St. Hubert and then to Moncton in April and May as a preliminary to commencing operations

from Yarmouth, Nova Scotia. However, the RCAF now decided that 8 (BR) would operate instead 18 Blenheim IV's ordered pre-war and shipped in May 1940, while 119 (BR), training on single-engined seaplanes on the West Coast, would operate the Bolingbrokes. The Blenheims, however, were no sooner unloaded at Halifax in June when, in response to British pleas, they were immediately shipped back to the UK. Then the 8 (BR) Bolingbroke detachment merged with 119 (BR), which now became the first operational Bolingbroke squadron, while 8 (BR)'s rump soldiered on with the Deltas.

By now the definitive Bolingbroke, the Mk.IV, (two Mk.I's had been converted to a II and a III) was in production. It had, among other new features, more powerful Mercury XV's, additional fuel tanks in the outer wings and a modified oil system. Not only had almost all

**It has often been stated that the Bolingbroke/Blenheim IV aerodynamic prototype K7072 was shipped to Canada at this time to serve "as a pattern aircraft." This is not the case. After serving as a prototype it was transferred to the Royal Aeronautical Establishment, Farnborough where it was engaged in de-icing trials. In late 1940 this program was transferred to Canada to be continued by the National Research Council. K7072 and Hudson T9305 were shipped to Canada in December 1940. K7072 was taken on RCAF strength at Rockcliffe in February 1941, when several well-known photos were taken which seems to have been the sole inspiration for the "pattern aircraft" myth.*

Right: Boly 9066 in the new Home War Establishment Anti-Submarine Aircraft paint scheme. Visible to the rear of the bomb bay doors in this view are the mounting points for the Light Series Stores Carriers usually carried by ASW-tasked Bolingbrokes and the starboard positioned trailing aerial fairlead. The freshly applied black Ubat marking is in commemoration of the aircraft's earlier, active combat days with 119 (BR) Squadron in Eastern Air Command. It never met an enemy vessel of any kind while with 147 (BR) Squadron.

Left: The original marking, applied over the aircraft's original factory finish in white next to the 119 (BR) RCAF badge.

non-Canadian components been eliminated, but the highly unsatisfactory cockpit interior and instrument layout had been completely redesigned.*** After an almost surreal process of indecision, order and counter-order, while 15 Mk.IVW's and 1 IVC were produced with P&W Twin Wasps and Wright Cyclones respectively, all other Mk.IV's had the Mercury XV. The first Bolingbroke IV's went to 8 (BR) in Sydney in early 1941. In late summer 1941 119 (BR), re-equipped with IVW's [see p.40], but soon exchanged them for Mk.IV's including 9066 which arrived on 13 November. 119 (BR) was the only RCAF squadron to be fully equipped successively with all three Bolingbroke production variants. Most Mk.I's were converted to fighters and issued to 115 (F), which took up residence at Patricia Bay, BC in October 1941.

*** Oddly enough, this last has usually been described as "American instrumentation" – a minor aspect of the redesign.*

As the aircraft supply situation became more difficult, the RCAF realized it would have to rely heavily on the Bolingbroke IV, though it was far from an ideal aircraft for its needs, and intentions were to have it in four EAC squadrons and also to replace Digby and Hudson attrition as well as to equip units in WAC. Fortunately, in September 1941, a shortage of Fairey Battles and their spares in the Bombing and Gunnery Schools of the BCATP enabled Canada to arrange an exchange whereby Bolingbrokes would be withdrawn from HWE squadrons and issued to the B&G Schools while Britain would supply 55 lend-lease

Hudsons for use by EAC units. A total of 151 Bolingbroke IV's IVW's and IVC's were built – many of the later examples going direct to the BCATP primarily for use as target tugs. In addition 457 Mk.IVT B&G trainers, making a total of 626 of all marks.

Diversion of Bolingbroke IV's to the BCATP was delayed by the entry of Japan into the war. 8 (BR) was rushed across the country in the depths of winter to WAC, 115 (F) exchanged its Bolingbroke IF's for IVF's and 147 (BR) was formed in WAC in July 1942.

While 13 (OT), 121 (K), 122 (K) and 163 (AC) squadrons all at one time or another had small numbers of Bolingbrokes on strength, there were only four operational Bolingbroke units. 119 (BR) continued using them in EAC

Bristol (Fairchild built) Bolingbroke Mk.IV 9066, Western Air Command, Patricia Bay, British Columbia, August 18, 1943.

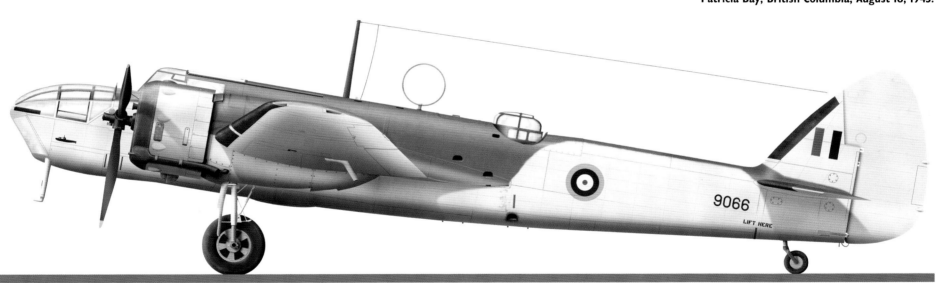

Following repair after its 28 August 1942 crash while with 147 (BR) Squadron, 9066 was refinished in the new RCAF Anti-submarine Warfare Aircraft camouflage scheme. This comprised almost entirely Matte White plus Dark Slate Grey and Extra Dark Sea Grey counter-highlight areas on the top surfaces of the wings, tail, and fuselage with national markings of smaller dimensions and no underwing markings. Although the 119 (BR) badge has been removed, a black U-boat attack marking, of slightly different pattern than the original, was reapplied. The more rotund shape (when compared to both nacelles on the Blenheim and the Bolingbroke's own starboard nacelle) of the port nacelle fairing is barely noticeable in this direct profile view — as the wing obscures the most affected portion — but is well in evidence in most photos. A unique feature of all Bolingbrokes except the Mk.IVWs, it extended further back over the top wing surface, and was differently tapered in both plan and profile, accommodating a dinghy and its inflation system in its rear part, as well as new oil system components in its forward part. A Bowden cable secured neatly along the wing trailing edge (with its handle in an orifice just visible below the second entry step) could be used by an escaping crew to pop the hatch, release the dinghy and inflate it, all with one pull. Similar lines went to a handle in the pilot's cockpit and a Walter Kidde impact-pressure actuator in the lower part of the port engine cowling. The turret is shown in the retracted cruise position, from which the guns could not be positioned or deployed and thus had to be stowed.

until June 1942, when it became fully operational on Hudsons. 115 (F) was moved with its Bolingbroke fighters to Annette Island, Alaska in April 1942. It switched to the BR role in June and operated from Annette until August 1943, when it returned to Pat Bay and re-equipped with Venturas. 8 (BR) was rushed north to Alaska in early June 1942 in response to the Japanese attack on the Aleutians. It became the RCAF's best-known Bolingbroke unit, operating from Anchorage, Kodiak and Nome, though it made no contact with the enemy. It returned to Canada in March 1943 and exchanged its Bolingbrokes for Venturas in May. 147 (BR) was the last Bolingbroke unit, still operating them from Tofino until disbanded in March 1944, with the

aging Bolingbrokes presenting increasing problems and hazards. When 119 (BR) switched to Hudsons our subject, 9066 became one of 147 (BR)'s first aircraft, but had a comparatively short career with that unit. On 28 August 1942 while returning from a search for Stranraer 951 it suffered engine trouble which resulted in a propeller and reduction gear flying off. The pilot, P/O Thomas, made a

successful forced landing with the bomb-loaded Bolingbroke in a field near Sea Island, incurring B category damage. 9066 was repaired and repainted, emerging in December 1942, but does not seem to have returned to 147 (BR), operating instead from Pat Bay on other duties. Sometime in September 1943 it went into storage and apparently saw no further active service.****

**** *One product of 9066's sojourn in WAC and the resulting photos is the theory that the sub-marking means it is the 115 (BR) Bolingbroke that was credited, along with ships of the US Coast Guard, with the destruction of a Japanese submarine which, for some reason, it identified as RO-32. The origin of the sub marking has been given above and, unfortunately, research has shown that no Japanese submarines were lost or even in these waters on that date, while RO-32 had been removed from the active list before Japan entered the war.*

Bolingbroke IV 9066 is shown here wearing what was likely her final paint scheme. This particular aircraft is also unique in having its usual football-fairing enclosed direction finding loop antenna replaced by a much larger diameter simple loop, possibly from another aircraft type (see also p.22 photo lower right). The reason for the change is unknown. The photo is dated 18 Aug. 1943, by which time the overall finish was well weathered to the extent that the reapplied Ubat marking has nearly worn off. External evidence of the Fairchild-built Bolingbroke's cold-weather gear include the wing and tail leading edge de-icer boots and heating intensifier pipes running through the cowl-mounted engine exhausts. These items are often overlooked, or at worst hidden, in most photos of the type as the Black / Green / Brown factory finish applied to operational Boly IVs resulted in very dark black and white images. *photo: LAC PBG4149*

Northrop Delta Bomber Reconnaissance Aircraft

…Oh Delta Aircraft, must you be a warrior bird? Oh, can't you see in beauty of your lines and length in trimness of your span, no strength…

This short excerpt from "Ode to the Delta" by B.B. Williams refers to the Northrop Deltas of 120 (BR) Squadron, RCAF, at Patricia Bay, BC and contains as much truth as poetry. The Delta which was then nearing the end of its operational career, had evolved from being an adequate photo survey aircraft developed from an excellent (at least by early '30's standards) fast light transport into a bomber reconnaissance seaplane that was simply not rugged enough for the duties imposed upon it. The illustrative portion of this AviaDossier examines the Delta at this point, but how did it happen?

The Delta, more than any other aircraft, epitomizes the RCAF's uneasy transition from a civil to a military air arm. In the decade and a half after WWI the RCAF and its predecessors, in order to justify their existence to penurious politicians and a disinterested populace, devoted most of its activity to civil government operations. Forestry and geological survey, fire patrol and suppression, crop and forest dusting, fishery and anti-smuggling patrol, aerial photography and mapping were some of the operations undertaken. In many of these the RCAF and Canada became world leaders, none more so than the last. Most of Canada's vast expanse was sketchily mapped, or, for the most part, totally unsurveyed. Directed and coordinated by all federal agencies concerned and using and developing the best photographic equipment and operational techniques, the RCAF was internationally respected. By the mid 1930's, however, even Canada could see that the world situation was changing, so that the RCAF was trying with a limited budget to become a military force while most of its civil activities had been discontinued or transferred. The one exception was photo survey and mapping.

In February 1935 the portentously titled Sub-Committee on Photographic Aircraft and Aerial Cameras – an interdepartmental body chaired by the National Research Council – determined that the RCAF would have to acquire a new photo aircraft. In the previous 15 years these had progressed from WWI types to wooden-hulled purpose-built flying boats and then to Fairchild and Bellanca bush planes on metal floats. The current type in use was the Bellanca CH-300 Pacemaker carrying an RCAF-designed triple camera mount for combined oblique and vertical photography. The sub-committee felt that the next aircraft must be larger, with increased range and higher performance. It considered eight aircraft – American, British and Canadian – and recommended two – photo versions of the Northrop Delta (to be built by Canadian Vickers) and the Fairchild Super 71. It was decided to order three of the former and two of the latter and determine subsequent acquisition by actual performance in the field. In the event, the Super 71P turned out to be a failure, so the Delta became the RCAF's last prewar photo aircraft.

The Delta was the fourth of a series of single-engine, low-wing monoplanes of metal stressed-skin construction designed by JK Northrop. As a transport with two crew members and ten passengers, its commercial success was curtailed by US legislation severely restricting the airline employment of single-engine passenger aircraft. Only nine were built by Northrop, with most of them having an extremely varied existence. It was the first aircraft with this construction to be built by Canadian Vickers, or, indeed, in Canada.

120(BR) Squadron's ramp and hangar at Pat Bay sometime in 1941. Our small tailed subject – Delta Mk.II 675 – is the aircraft closest to the photographer while the next two Deltas feature the uniquely Canadian big tail. The length of rope (or cable?) hanging off the tailwheel axle and lack of a handling dolly, wheeled fore and aft, (normally part of the beaching gear for float planes) seems to be *de rigueur* for parked Delta float planes. The black area often seen on the wing of some Deltas, such as 686 MX•F here, is a clip-on removeable wing walk and not the usual black anti-skid coating. Note the position and style of the upper wing roundels. Though the float installation had its problems, once in level flight the aircraft had proved to be an excellent photo survey platform.

The Canadian Vickers aircraft department was at a very low ebb during the Depression (although it had built six Bellanca CH-300 Pacemakers for the RCAF). It was short-staffed with poor facilities and the Delta order was a blessing. The first Deltas had to be almost handmade, but no major problems were encountered*. The task may have been simplified by the fact that the fuselage was constructed in two sections, top and bottom, which allowed installation of wires, controls and equipment before assembly. There were many changes to fit the Delta for its new role: fewer windows, a very large upward-opening freight door in the port side, a strengthened cabin floor and apertures and fittings for the triple mount, with three Fairchild A-3 cameras, which had been designed for the Bellancas. The RCAF had considered including attachments so that passenger seats could be installed but decided against it. The contract required that the Delta must pass acceptance tests on wheels, skis and floats, though its main work would be done on floats. Canadian Vickers designed floats – the Model 75 – specifically for the Delta. While the aircraft should have been ready by 31 March 1936, material shortages and manufacturing difficulties delayed completion and the first of the three Deltas (serials 667, 668 and 669) was not ready until late August, completing its manufacturer's flight test on floats on 1 September and being flown to Ottawa for RCAF acceptance later that month. The other two were delivered in October and November and after tests on floats and wheels were accepted subject to some minor alterations. After these were completed on Delta 667, it was issued to No. 6 (GP) Detachment of 8 (GP) Squadron for camera installation, calibration and testing. It was found superior in almost every way to the Bellanca with good visibility, stability and performance. The only adverse feature was that the pilot's downward visibility over the immediate area being photographed being poor. One unexpected fault was discovered soon after – a dangerously high level of carbon monoxide during photo operations from exhaust fumes entering the camera ports. Temporary screening and ventilating measures were adopted until a new exhaust system could be developed.

By late November 1936, the RCAF had determined that the Delta was going to be its photo aircraft and prepared to order another four. While the RCAF knew that the Delta could be used for military purposes, this had not been a consideration when the first three were ordered. It was now felt that RCAF Deltas should be convertible to "seaplane bombers" as their performance was adequate for "maintenance of neutrality" operations. The specifications for the new aircraft were amended both to rectify problems observed in the first three and to provide for rapid conversion to military uses. Some of the former included a new exhaust system, a new oil cooler with a prominent outlet, fabric replacing the metal rudder covering, new shock absorbers with increased travel, additional cockpit windows immediately beneath the existing ones, and an oval window in the bottom forward fuselage for the pilot. The latter included a window for a prone-position bomb aimer, provision for bomb carriers under the wings and fuselage, for a fixed gun in each wing and for a gunner's hatch in the upper and in the lower rear fuselage. The first three Deltas were now designated Mark I and the four on order (serials 670 to 673) Mark II. These were delivered to the RCAF in November 1937. Four additional Mk.II's were ordered in June 1937, followed by a further order for nine in November.

In the meantime, while 668 remained at Rockcliffe for various trials and tests, 6 (GP) Detachment left on 18 April 1937 for British Columbia, flying 667 and 669 as landplanes across the US to Seattle and then to Vancouver where they converted to floats. They spent the next six months making photo survey flights from Prince Rupert and various Vancouver Island sites. 669's season was briefly interrupted in May when it sank at its moorings. It was raised, dried out, fitted with new floats and put back into service. This incident was the first of the sinkings that would happen with regrettable frequency. A combination of the Model 75 float's construction, material and sealing and the Delta's tail-down floating attitude meant that, until the Delta was

text continued on p.28

On 2 November 1941, a 5 (BR) pilot, who had just delivered a Stranraer [see p.38] to WAC was being checked out on Delta 690 prior to delivering it to Fingal, Ontario, on his way back east. Unfamiliarity with the type caused him to ground-loop and nose over the Delta on landing. This unusual point of view provides a rare glimpse at underside details like the sliding hatch over the main camera port (mid-fuselage), trailing aerial fairlead (to starboard of camera hatch), empty Light Series Stores Carrier adapter rails under each wing, landing/taxi lights, deployed flaps, and the spacing between the ailerons and the rear cell wall of the wing. The ground crew appear to be recovering spilled fuel while an armed guard looks on.

photo: LAC PA125811

It has been stated that the final Northrop-built Delta, model 1 D-8 s/n 185, went to Canadian Vickers to act as a pattern for the RCAF machines, and even that Northrop-built components were used in these aircraft (despite this being forbidden in the contract). There is no reference to this in RCAF records or in the recollections of Canadian Vickers employees. Certainly the RCAF did not pay for it and it is doubtful that Canadian Vickers could afford to. In the absence of more definite documentation it would appear to be another "pattern aircraft" myth.

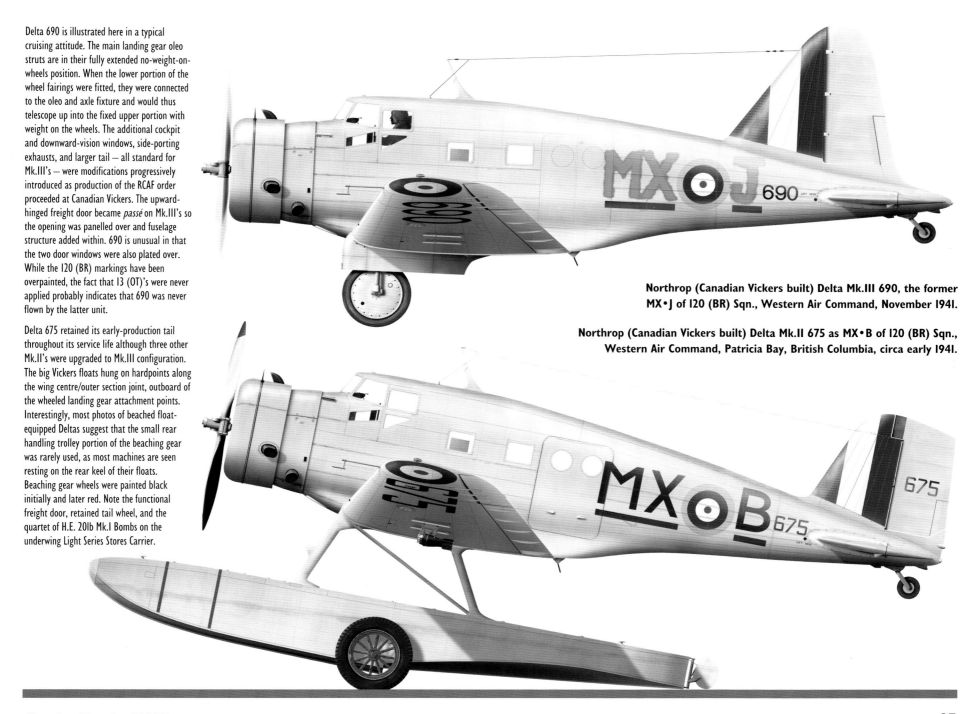

Delta 690 is illustrated here in a typical cruising attitude. The main landing gear oleo struts are in their fully extended no-weight-on-wheels position. When the lower portion of the wheel fairings were fitted, they were connected to the oleo and axle fixture and would thus telescope up into the fixed upper portion with weight on the wheels. The additional cockpit and downward-vision windows, side-porting exhausts, and larger tail — all standard for Mk.III's — were modifications progressively introduced as production of the RCAF order proceeded at Canadian Vickers. The upward-hinged freight door became *passé* on Mk.III's so the opening was panelled over and fuselage structure added within. 690 is unusual in that the two door windows were also plated over. While the 120 (BR) markings have been overpainted, the fact that 13 (OT)'s were never applied probably indicates that 690 was never flown by the latter unit.

Delta 675 retained its early-production tail throughout its service life although three other Mk.II's were upgraded to Mk.III configuration. The big Vickers floats hung on hardpoints along the wing centre/outer section joint, outboard of the wheeled landing gear attachment points. Interestingly, most photos of beached float-equipped Deltas suggest that the small rear handling trolley portion of the beaching gear was rarely used, as most machines are seen resting on the rear keel of their floats. Beaching gear wheels were painted black initially and later red. Note the functional freight door, retained tail wheel, and the quartet of H.E. 20lb Mk.I Bombs on the underwing Light Series Stores Carrier.

Northrop (Canadian Vickers built) Delta Mk.III 690, the former MX•J of 120 (BR) Sqn., Western Air Command, November 1941.

Northrop (Canadian Vickers built) Delta Mk.II 675 as MX•B of 120 (BR) Sqn., Western Air Command, Patricia Bay, British Columbia, circa early 1941.

withdrawn from service four years later, they were liable to sink while moored. When 667 and 669 returned from BC in November 1937 they were, with 668, immediately flown to Canadian Vickers for conversion to full Mark II standard.

The next year saw six Deltas (667 and 669, 668 and 670, 672 and 673) sent into the field with three detachments of 8 (GP) Squadron. Delta 671 was retained at Rockcliffe for various trials and tests, including armament. In the latter only ground and flight performance trials with a bomb load and the fixed gun were carried out [Note: no Delta ever carried more than one fixed gun, in the port wing]. Ski trials were also undertaken – while the four Mk.II's had flown with skis that winter, problems with the internal trimming feature were frequent. Indeed, this problem was never overcome. The field operations were comparatively uneventful except that, on 14 June 1938 in northern Saskatchewan, Delta 672 went into an involuntary spin and recovered after losing 3000 feet (915 m) of altitude. The incident was initially attributed to slipped aileron cables. In late 1938 the next four Delta II's, 674-677 were delivered. The first of the next nine, 682, started trials in November, but winter conditions delayed final acceptance until January 1939.

The final stages of RCAF Delta redesign and modification are rather complex and have been the subject of much confusion and misinterpretation. Space prohibits more than a brief summary. In early 1939 it was decided to complete the remaining eight Deltas for bomber reconnaissance rather than photographic duties. While 673 went to Trenton for bombing and gunnery trials, which were successful except for the ventral gun which was useless and soon abandoned, construction of these eight was delayed until the RCAF completed the design of a dorsal gun position. In June 1939 this was fitted to 672, after its freight door had been plated over to strengthen the fuselage. As well as the opening and gun ring an immense curved windscreen was fitted. This installation caused severe fin buffeting in some flight modes, so, with NRC assistance, first a conical, then a turtle-back fairing was developed, extending from the gun position to half-way along the upper rear fuselage, which largely eliminated the problem. It was decided to modify all existing Deltas to this configuration and 1 Aircraft Depot, Ottawa, started work in August 1939. The final eight Deltas were now to be fitted with a turret (whether manual or power is unclear) and Canadian Vickers started work on a fuselage mockup for this installation.

The other factor that triggered Delta re-design was perceived in early 1939, when another Delta went into a spin, this time in a blizzard, but recovered. The RCAF concluded that the Delta was spin prone and, as a "quick-fix" decided to fit anti-spin parachutes in the tail cones of all existing aircraft while, with data from the NRC wind tunnel, the vertical tail would be redesigned. The result was a much larger fin and rudder, located further forward on the fuselage, giving the false impression of an extended tail cone. Part of the redesign was a ventral fin which, proving to have insufficient ground clearance, was removed in landplane configuration, but retained when the Deltas were on floats. Before this design had even been finalized, 8 (GP) had gone to war. On 22 September 1939, one of the two Deltas, 672 and 670, so far fitted with the dorsal gun position which had rendered their performance "deplorably inadequate," developed a 6-inch fracture in the area of the gun ring. This was the last straw for the RCAF, which totally abandoned the dorsal gun concept, ordered work stopped on conversion (which left 668 and 682 without freight doors), the dorsal positions removed from 670 and 672 and Canadian Vickers to drop the turret mock-up and complete the remaining Deltas with simply a small observer's hatch in the dorsal position. The delays caused by the armament indecisiveness and redesigned tail meant that the final eight Deltas – 683 to 690 – were not completed until 1940. Also converted to the new configuration were 676, which served as a prototype and the elderly 667 and 668, all three of which were at Canadian Vickers for restoration following operational damage.** Interestingly, when trials revealed that the new empennage had solved the spinning problem, the RCAF did not install the anti-spin parachutes in the tails of the Mk.III's, while the Mk.II's retained them.

In mid-summer 1939, 8 (GP) had only five Deltas out on photo operations, two of which were surveying the coast of Labrador for potential bases. The others were at Rockcliffe with the Test and Development Flight or awaiting installation of the dorsal gun position, while 675 was leading a peripatetic

Above: A rare airborne photograph of an RCAF Delta. This one also shows 689's Mk.III standard roof hatch that replaced the proposed upper gun position. The ventral fixture — more "fairing" than "fin" — was retained by the big-tailed Deltas whenever they were operated on floats. Note that the tail-wheel strut and axle remain installed.

Right: Another view of the float-equipped 689 at Pat Bay. The rarely used rear trolley part of the beaching gear is lashed to the rear of the starboard float. The length of rope hanging from the tail-wheel axle seems to be a common feature of beached Delta floatplanes.

existence after serving earlier that year with 1 (F) squadron giving potential Hurricane pilots experience of a quasi-modern monoplane. Then, on 24 August, 8 (BR) was ordered to recall all detached aircraft and on the 26th and 27th seven Deltas left for Nova Scotia. All were at the new base at Sydney by 28 August except for 673, which, after experiencing engine trouble on several occasions en route disappeared on 14 September over New Brunswick. The wreck was not found until 1958, and now is held by the National Aeronautical Collection, Ottawa. From Sydney, where the facilities were, at first, literally non-existent, 8 (GP), later redesignated 8 (BR), commenced Delta operations – patrols, escorts and coastal reconnaissance – as far afield as southern Newfoundland. At first flying from the Sydney River base and later from Kelly Beach near North Sydney, all RCAF Delta II's except 675 and the late 673 served with 8 (BR), often briefly. While reasonably reliable in the air, the Delta was exceptionally fragile on the water. Landing, taking off or just taxiing in any kind of swell cause rivets to pop and strains or fractures to occur in the wing web structure near the float attachment. By October 1940 damage of this nature, varying in seriousness, had been sustained by six Deltas – 676, 670, 668, 682, 677 and 667. In addition, leaking floats caused a rash of sinkings until 8 (BR) discovered that leaving the flaps partially down when the Deltas were moored caused the force of the wind to make them ride nose down so that less water entered at the rear of the floats.

**Delta Marks have been subject to confusion.

- *Mark I: this was allotted to the first three aircraft, 667, 668 and 669 as originally constructed.*

- *Mark IA: this was a tentative designation for a version of the Mark I rebuilt to partial Mark II standard – i.e. without armament provision. After examining costs, the RCAF opted for a full Mark II rebuild, so the Mark IA never existed. This has not, however, prevented some sources from assuming that it did.*

- *Mark II: this was allotted to*

a) Deltas 670-677, 682 as constructed incorporating various improvements, modifications and provision for armament;

b) Deltas 667-669 as rebuilt over the winter of 1937-38 to the same standard as the above.

- *Mark III: this was allotted to:*

a) Deltas 683-690 as constructed with redesigned empennage, no freight door and small dorsal observer's hatch.

b) Deltas 676, 667, 668, which were Mark II's rebuilt to this standard. 676 was prototype for this mark.

Note: Some sources claim that Mark III was an "unofficial" designation. All RCAF and Canadian Vickers documentation, including technical drawings, that identify these aircraft by mark refer to them as Mark III. It is certainly an official designation.

Northrop Delta Mk.III 689 as MX•H of 120 (BR) Sqn., Western Air Command, Patricia Bay, British Columbia, early 1941.

The Canadian Vickers built Deltas were painted overall aluminum lacquer on a zinc chromate base [possibly red oxide primer on the first few]. Most aircraft appear to have been expertly finished as, with the exception of some scuffing down to the zinc chromate and underlying metal of the float sides and bottoms evident in various photos, the paint appears to have stayed generally intact throughout the type's RCAF service life. With its many rivets and longitudinal panel joints however, it was inevitable that these protrusions and crevices picked up exhaust, dirt and grime.

Northrop Delta Mk.III 685 as AN•P of 13 (OT) Sqn., Western Air Command, Patricia Bay, British Columbia, mid to late 1941.

685 was the third aircraft constructed from the beginning as a Mk.III. Unlike 690, the two round windows on the opposite side (where the freight door used to be) were retained. The high quality finish shows signs of the long term osmosis of dirt and grime. This is also evident in the photo below where the operational aircraft serial number has been overpainted and replaced by an instructional airframe serial. The AN•P markings are from 13(OT) Squadron, the unit that inherited (but rarely flew) a number of ex-120(BR) Deltas prior to their being handed over to the ground crew training school at St. Thomas, Ontario. Delta 685 was coded MX•E when with 120 (BR) Squadron.

It was the RCAF's initial wartime intention to equip two former Reserve squadrons with Deltas, 119 (BR) and 120 (BR). The former would have the Mk.II's after 8 (BR) had re-equipped with Bolingbrokes and the latter would receive the new Mk.III's. In the event, 119 (BR) got the Bolingbrokes (though it did operate Delta 670 for a month) while 8 (BR), missing out on Bolingbrokes and then Blenheims [for this story see p.22], continued with a few Deltas into the winter of 1940/41 until finally thankfully converting to Bolingbrokes. 120 (BR) did, indeed, receive all the Delta III's, both new and converted, except 684. This spent its entire operational career with the Test and Development Flight in Ottawa, the only

Delta never to serve with a squadron. 120 (BR) also operated Mk.II's 670 and 675. This squadron undertook patrols and training from Sea Island and Patricia Bay between June 1940 and July 1941, but was essentially marking time until more suitable aircraft arrived. The Delta's seaworthiness was only marginally better in the Pacific than in the Atlantic, and the floats leaked as much as ever. A cure for this seems to have been found in March 1941 just as it was decided to operate the Deltas exclusively as landplanes.

That month, 120 (BR) began to receive Hudsons (though it soon reverted to flying boats) and started to transfer the Deltas

to 13 (OT) Squadron, which found very little use for them. They became hangar queens, only a few ever flying, taking up valuable space. RCAF HQ racked its collective brains trying to find a way to put them to use, but could not, and all offers to various HWE and BCATP Commands were politely refused. Also, the Deltas had evolved so far from their civilian form that they were commercially unsalable. Finally, it was considered that their best contribution to the war effort would be as instructional airframes. Thus in late 1941 the majority of the surviving Deltas were flown or shipped to Fingal, Ontario, from whence they entered the maw of the huge Technical Training School at St. Thomas, never to emerge.***

*** *Instructional Airframes:*
These were aircraft that remained on RCAF strength but were designated as unflyable and used, for the most part, for training ground personnel such as mechanics, riggers and fitters in maintenance and repair. Usually they were obsolete types and models or had been damaged and deemed irreparable. Most of the aircraft with which the RCAF entered the war ended up as instructional airframes. Because of the use to which they were put few survived the war to be declared surplus. These airframes were identified by a consecutive series of "A" prefixed numbers.

Although the instructional airframe serial A149 has already been applied, the setting suggests the photo was taken when the Delta was en route to Fingal, Ontario.

photo: John Melson collection

Douglas **Boston III** Intruder Aircraft

Hush ye, Hush ye, dinna fret ye; the Black Douglas willna get ye. This "lullaby" supposedly sung by 14th century English mothers anent a Scottish peer of swarthy complexion and sanguinary proclivities might well have been echoed by *Luftwaffe* air and ground personnel in 1942/43. The reference now was to the black Douglas Boston III intruders of 418 Squadron, RCAF.

The gestation process by which the initial Douglas 7 concept of a three-place twin-engined light bomber in 1936 evolved into the intruder aircraft that 418 flew in 1942/43 is complicated. To summarize, it first flew as the Model 7B in late 1938 and, after a major redesign, emerged as the DB-7 in 1939 with major French, and later British, orders for both the original DB-7 and the later DB-7A. After the fall of France Britain took over the remainder of the French order and these aircraft, known to the RAF as Havocs, were employed from late 1940 as intruders and night fighters. In the latter role, because of its size and power, it was equipped with radar and was selected to inaugurate two of Fighter Command's most imaginative (not to say bizarre) concepts. They were the Long Aerial Mine, an explosive device towed at the end of a 2000 foot (610 m) cable in the hope that the cable could be manoeuvred in front of a German bomber, and the Turbinlite, a 2,700 million candle-power searchlight in the Havoc's nose with which it could illuminate an enemy aircraft while a pair of accompanying Hurricanes shot it down. Both schemes had negligible success.

Meanwhile, the basic design underwent a progressive process of development – redesigned tail surfaces, more powerful engines, increased armament and bombload – and served throughout the war. It flew with the USAAF as the A-20 attack aircraft and P-70 night fighter, and, now renamed Boston, with the RAF, RAAF and SAAF and other allied services. Over 3,000, nearly half the total produced, served with the Soviet Naval and Red Army Air Forces. Only three reached Canada where they came on RCAF strength for a short time while they were used for chemical warfare trials at Suffield, Alberta. Most of the type's wartime service was as a light bomber and ground attack aircraft, but it was quite frequently given a role more traditionally that of a fighter. One such was that of intruder – a concept developed by the RAF during the German night bomber offensive of 1940-41 whereby fighters – initially Hurricanes, but later Havocs - would orbit the German bases at night, hoping to catch the bombers on their return. By 1942 the RAF was doing the bombing and the aim of the intruders was to handicap the *Luftwaffe's* night fighters by attacking them while landing, or, failing this, by bombing the runways and installations. At first the RAF intruder force was small – the most suitable aircraft, Havocs and Bostons, were needed in other roles – but with the arrival of the Mosquito mid-war it went from strength to strength.

418 (City of Edmonton) Squadron RCAF, the only squadron specifically formed as an intruder unit, was created at Debden, Essex on 15 November 1941. The aircrew cadre was a nucleus, which included some Canadians, from 23 RAF Intruder Squadron, including some Canadians, plus RCAF volunteers. By 11 February 1942, 418 had reached its full establishment of 18 Boston III's, all new aircraft. After intensive training, often in very bad weather, to familiarize the crews with their aircraft, their role and with each other, during which two aircraft and one crew were lost, the squadron was declared operational on 22 March 1942.

The squadron's first operation on 27 March was not an intruder mission but a night-bombing raid on oil refineries near Ghent in Belgium. Eight Bostons each took a 1000 pound (455 kg) payload. The next night, however, six Bostons undertook classic intruder operations over Dutch and French airfields. After that, 418 never looked back. Night after night, sometimes singly, sometimes in pairs, the Bostons took off, their target German night fighter airfields. Hurtling across the Channel at 150 feet (46 m) to avoid the radar, they would zoom to 4000 feet (1200 m), dive through

Boston W8268 "O for Ottawa" failed to return on 20 May 1942 from an operation against the *Luftwaffe* airfield at Soesterberg, Netherlands, in support of a Bomber Command attack on Mannheim. The crew, P/O Stabb (RAF), P/O Riches and F/Sgt Duxfield (RCAF) are buried at Amersfoort, Netherlands. Although this aircraft has sometimes been portrayed as having a 20mm gun pack, it was never fitted with this installation, owing to its loss prior to these coming into use on 418 Sqn Bostons. The silhouette of the engine nacelle in several of the existing photos of this aircraft, as seen here, may have led to this assumption.

photo: LAC PL7718

the flak belt and then fly figure-8 orbits at 1000 feet (305 m) around the airfield, hoping to catch a victim during the brief period its lights and the runway lights were on. The Germans were often aware of the intruder's presence, and with great ingenuity employed dummy lights, airstrips and aircraft, decoy lights and aircraft plus flak traps and their own fighters to divert or destroy the enemy. It was a constant battle of wits. The Bostons' activity was often tied to that of Bomber Command – if a major raid was scheduled, the intruders would be required that night. For Operation Millennium, the 1000-bomber Cologne raid, 19 Bostons of 23 and 418 squadrons were deployed against all known night-fighter airfields along the route. In mid-May 1942, 418 received its first Boston III intruders refitted with four 20mm cannon underneath the fuselage [reported as the Intruder III configuration – ed].

Flying from Debden and, later, from Bradwell Bay (April 1942) and Ford (April 1943), 418 operated Bostons for a year and a quarter. It suffered a steady string of operational losses – the first on 27 April when P/O Askwith and crew failed to return in Z2240. That was the fate of a small but steady procession of Bostons over the next year – including two, W8231 and W8268 ("O for Ottawa") on 20 May 1942. One sad aspect of this was that for the most part their fate – faulty navigation, mechanical failure, enemy action – was never discovered. There was also the usual run of accidents – for example, the Bostons were extremely prone to undercarriage failure. The squadron's first claims against enemy aircraft were on 26 April when P/O Harding and crew claimed a Ju88 damaged and 7 May when P/O Lucas caught an enemy fighter taxiing at Gilze-Rijen and destroyed it with bombs.

418's operational priority during its Boston days remained the handicapping of the enemy night fighter force, though it occasionally did a little leaflet dropping and, far more exciting and effective, night train-busting. The 20mm cannon proved particularly devastating except when they jammed or froze – a habit that bothered the 418 armament men, until a Fighter Command expert told them it was not their fault but freezing due to the extremely poor insulation of the belly gun pack.

Although the squadron's first Mosquito arrived on 18 February 1943, the Bostons carried much of the operational load for another four months, claiming a number of enemy aircraft destroyed or damaged – the last one being a Do217 probably destroyed over St. Dizier on 20 June. From May through July the Bostons were gradually ferried away to be reconverted to bombers. 418 went on to become the RCAF's highest scoring squadron of WWII. While most of

photos: top – LAC PL15889
bottom LAC PL15875

Bostons, Havocs, and Intruders:
While the RAF designation for the Douglas DB-7B bomber and the very similar A-20C was Boston III and IIIA respectively, and although officially redesignated as Havoc III for the intruder role, service personnel stuck with the popular title of Boston.

Intruder designated the role rather than the aircraft. Intruder I conversion sets changed earlier Boston I's into Havoc I's while the Intruder II counterpart, whether retaining the bomb bay or adding the later cannon pack converted Boston III and IIIA bombers to intruders. In addition, these aircraft incorporated such RAF modifications as personal relief tubes and the windshield glycol spray unit initially fitted to the solid-nosed Havoc II night fighter.

this carnage was committed by Mosquitoes, the squadron had learned its trade on the Black Douglas.

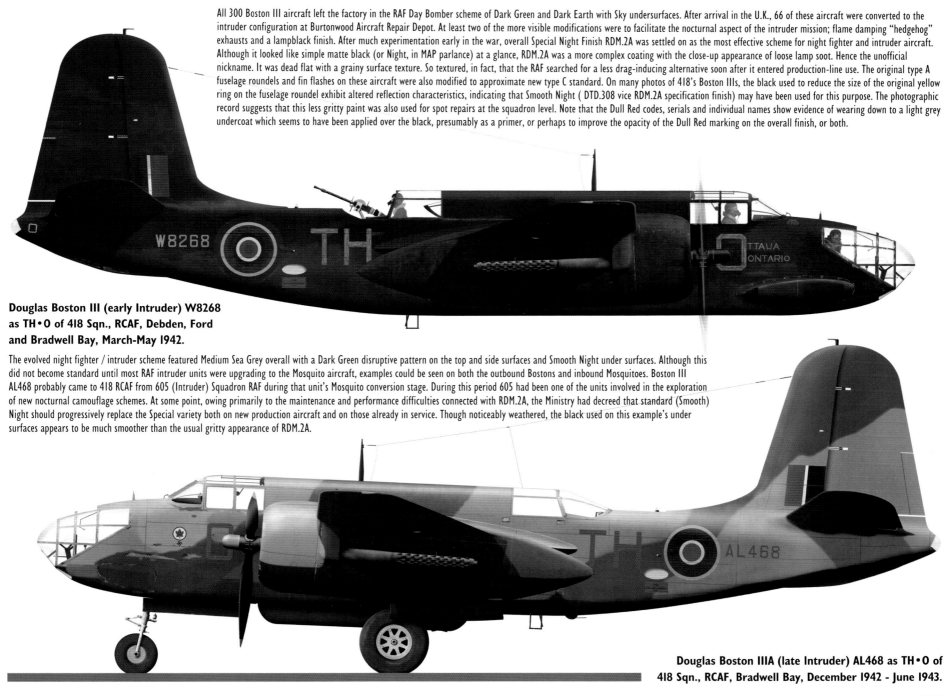

All 300 Boston III aircraft left the factory in the RAF Day Bomber scheme of Dark Green and Dark Earth with Sky undersurfaces. After arrival in the U.K., 66 of these aircraft were converted to the intruder configuration at Burtonwood Aircraft Repair Depot. At least two of the more visible modifications were to facilitate the nocturnal aspect of the intruder mission; flame damping "hedgehog" exhausts and a lampblack finish. After much experimentation early in the war, overall Special Night Finish RDM.2A was settled on as the most effective scheme for night fighter and intruder aircraft. Although it looked like simple matte black (or Night, in MAP parlance) at a glance, RDM.2A was a more complex coating with the close-up appearance of loose lamp soot. Hence the unofficial nickname. It was dead flat with a grainy surface texture. So textured, in fact, that the RAF searched for a less drag-inducing alternative soon after it entered production-line use. The original type A fuselage roundels and fin flashes on these aircraft were also modified to approximate new type C standard. On many photos of 418's Boston IIIs, the black used to reduce the size of the original yellow ring on the fuselage roundel exhibit altered reflection characteristics, indicating that Smooth Night (DTD.308 vice RDM.2A specification finish) may have been used for this purpose. The photographic record suggests that this less gritty paint was also used for spot repairs at the squadron level. Note that the Dull Red codes, serials and individual names show evidence of wearing down to a light grey undercoat which seems to have been applied over the black, presumably as a primer, or perhaps to improve the opacity of the Dull Red marking on the overall finish, or both.

**Douglas Boston III (early Intruder) W8268
as TH•O of 4l8 Sqn., RCAF, Debden, Ford
and Bradwell Bay, March-May 1942.**

The evolved night fighter / intruder scheme featured Medium Sea Grey overall with a Dark Green disruptive pattern on the top and side surfaces and Smooth Night under surfaces. Although this did not become standard until most RAF intruder units were upgrading to the Mosquito aircraft, examples could be seen on both the outbound Bostons and inbound Mosquitoes. Boston III AL468 probably came to 418 RCAF from 605 (Intruder) Squadron RAF during that unit's Mosquito conversion stage. During this period 605 had been one of the units involved in the exploration of new nocturnal camouflage schemes. At some point, owing primarily to the maintenance and performance difficulties connected with RDM.2A, the Ministry had decreed that standard (Smooth) Night should progressively replace the Special variety both on new production aircraft and on those already in service. Though noticeably weathered, the black used on this example's under surfaces appears to be much smoother than the usual gritty appearance of RDM.2A.

**Douglas Boston IIIA (late Intruder) AL468 as TH•O of
418 Sqn., RCAF, Bradwell Bay, December 1942 - June 1943.**

Consolidated
Liberator GR.V (Can)
Maritime Patrol Aircraft

It was nearly mid-day and Liberator 595 X of 10 (BR) Squadron, RCAF, was 250 miles (402 km) south of the Virgin Rocks on the Grand Banks, returning from a convoy escort, when a U-boat was sighted, running full speed on the surface. As the Liberator went in to attack, the U-boat ran up a black flag while crewmen ran up to the conning tower frantically waving their hands. The aircraft flashed the signal *Halten Warteband* (Stop and Wait) and flew guard on U-889 until ships from an RCN Escort Group arrived to accept its surrender. It way 10 May 1945, the curtain was coming down on WWII's longest battle, the Battle of the Atlantic, and it was fitting that an aircraft of a type that, more than any other, was responsible for an Allied victory, was in at the end in the western Atlantic.

The Liberator GR.V (Canada) has a significance in the history of Canadian military aviation greater than the number acquired (15) would indicate. The Liberator was undoubtedly the most successful anti-submarine aircraft of WWII. Its acquisition finally gave the RCAF an effective machine for that role with oceanic range and state-of-the-art electronics and weaponry. From then on Eastern Air Command ceased to be the Cinderella air service in the Battle of the Atlantic.

Space prohibits more than a brief summary of the RCAF's acquisition of the aircraft. Suffice it to say that by late 1942 the handful of Liberator I's operated by the RAF had, with their unique combination of range, speed and warload, proved to be phenomenally successful in the anti-sub role. In the teeth of resistance from Bomber Command, despite the U-boat offensive's success, Coastal Command had succeeded in getting an allocation of Liberators, first the GR.III and later the GR.V, both based on the B-24D. The type's inherent qualities, modern radar and weaponry, combined with tactical experience and good electronic intelligence made it the finest anti-sub aircraft in existence. The RCAF had long coveted the Liberator without success, but finally, at the Allied Convoy Conference in March 1943 and with considerable competition from the RAF, USAAF and USN, received an allocation of fifteen of the latest version.

These were delivered between 14 April and 27 May 1943 carrying the RAF serials BZ725 to BZ756, which, within a month, were changed to RCAF serials 586 to 600. While they had been diverted from an RAF Lend-Lease allocation, they were paid for by Canada under Canpay CA00076. Designated Liberator GR.V (Canada),* they differed from the RAF GR.V in armament – Consolidated twin .50 tail turret, .50 beam hatch guns, .50 ventral tunnel gun and .50 nose gun instead of the RAF Boulton Paul four .303 tail turret, .303 beam guns, no tunnel gun and initially, no nose gun, as well as a Minneapolis-Honeywell autopilot instead of the RAF's Sperry A-3, plus other minor difference. Thirteen had American-produced ASG centimetric radar in a 'Dumbo' radome under the nose, two had it in a retractable ventral housing, later replaced by a Dumbo.

text continued on p.36

* These aircraft have often been referred to as GR.III's, GR.V's or even GR.III/V's! This error is based on the RCAF inventory cards, which were the main source for the authoritative and invaluable book, RCAF Aircraft – Serials & Photographs. Unfortunately these cards were created and maintained by clerical staff who often designated aircraft by guesswork rather than documentation – as in this case.

Though not accredited with actual sinkings, Liberator GR.V (Can) 595 X, contributed to the successful crossings of convoys ONS18 and ONS202 on 22 September 1943 by engaging U-boats U-377 and U-402 in mid-Atlantic combat. Although the sinking of an enemy sub was the ultimate goal of such engagements, keeping them busy defending themselves, making them stay submerged, or sending them back to base for repairs were also very real victories in the ASW war, saving untold numbers of merchant vessels and warships plus their crews to contribute further to the allied victory. *photo: LAC PL21758*

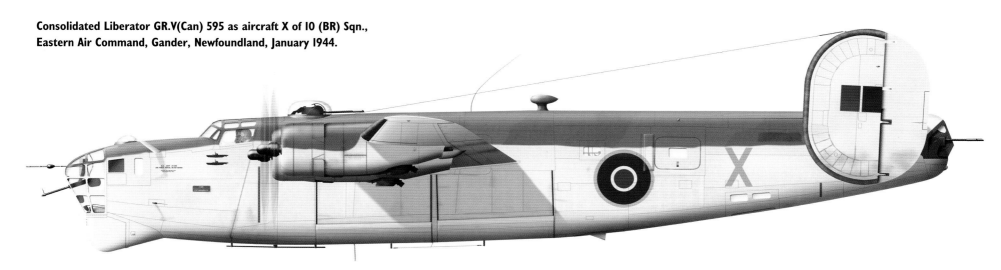

**Consolidated Liberator GR.V(Can) 595 as aircraft X of I0 (BR) Sqn.,
Eastern Air Command, Gander, Newfoundland, January 1944.**

Built with the USAAF serial 42-40469, Liberator 595 was originally earmarked for the RAF as Liberator GR.V BZ735. Soon after delivery to Canada (presumably when payment to the US had been arranged) the British serial was painted out on each side of the fuselage so that the proper RCAF serials could be applied. Like all early maritime patrol equipped Liberators destined for the RAF, 595 featured the Temperate Sea Scheme of Dark Slate Grey and Extra Dark Sea Grey upper surfaces with White sides and undersides. Also like their RAF Coastal Command counterparts, Eastern Air Command's Liberators did not carry roundels on the lower wing surfaces. Larger roundels (70" as opposed to the RAF's 54") were applied to the upper surfaces. Though the large areas of white on the airframe often gave the impression, at a distance, of a very clean finish, the paint on these GR.Vs was known to flake and chip with relative ease. The author's archival research uncovered official correspondence which suggested that the problem was due to the manufacturer not priming the aircraft properly prior to applying the topcoat of camouflage colours. The tail turrets on all I0 (BR) Squadron GR.V(Can) aircraft were in a different finish than the rest of the paint scheme, presumably the factory's standard USAAF Olive Drab. Note that the illustration shows the Browning .50 calibre M2 machine gun installed in the nose: Though not fitted during the convoy battles of 1943, it was definitely present by the time the two Ubat mission markers were added to the nose. *photo: LAC PL21757*

The first, and only, unit to use the GR.V (Can.)'s was 10 (Bomber Reconnaissance) Squadron. 10 (BR) had started the war with the archaic Westland Wapiti and had converted to the Douglas Digby, which it had flown since 1940. It was the RCAF's most experienced BR squadron with one confirmed kill (U-520) to its credit. Operating from Gander until November 1942, it moved to Dartmouth, Nova Scotia only to return to Gander in late April 1943 to convert to the Liberators. In addition to the squadron's existing personnel, EAC had been combed for outstanding air and ground crew to fill the larger establishment.

They worked hard converting to the Liberator, first at Dorval, then Gander. By 18 May eight crews were fully operational and, by June 10 (BR) was well into normal routine. As a Very Long Range (VLR) squadron, the Liberators were out ten to fifteen hours, flying convoy escorts, patrols and sub searches. Instrument flying, navigation and coping with abominable weather were taken in stride by the 10 (BR) aircrews. In order to wring the maximum range out of the Liberator by reducing weight the crew armour was removed and the armament was drastically reduced to the point where, in late summer, only the mid-upper turret guns remained. This was not as short-sighted as it may appear. Up to this time U-boats did not fight it out and their AA armament was negligible. By the end of the summer, however, the tail guns and port beam guns had been re-installed and a new nose gun position by the end of 1943.

10 (BR)'s Liberators went into service during a lull in the Battle of the Atlantic. The U-boats had suffered a resounding defeat in May 1943 and had been withdrawn from the North Atlantic except for a half dozen to keep the Allies occupied. On 3 July, 500 miles (805 km) NE of Newfoundland, while screening a convoy, P/O RR Stevenson followed up a radar contact in 587 B and, by

skilful use of cloud cover, took U-420 completely by surprise, dropping all ten depth charges in three attacks, while the mid-upper gunner rained fire on the sub. U-420 was severely damaged and limped back to base with two men dead and one wounded. Also in July 10 (BR) started to fill its role of covering the Black Pit – its aircraft went as far as Iceland and Northern Ireland and even flew several operations from the latter.

It was September 1943 that saw the squadron's greatest battle. The wolf-packs returned to the North Atlantic armed with acoustic torpedoes to deal with escort ships and a greatly augmented AA armament plus orders to fight it out on the surface with aircraft. On 19 September *Gruppe Leuthen* with 19 U-boats was in mid-Atlantic attempting to intercept two westbound convoys when F/L RF Fisher in Liberator 586 A sighted and attacked U-341. The aircraft was too high on the first pass and was hit on the wingtip by fierce flak, Fisher came round again and with six accurate depth charges put U-341 down. These and four more in the area where it submerged, destroyed the submarine.

For the next two days the two merged convoys and their escort fought their way westward, suffering losses at night when Iceland-based Liberators of 120 Squadron, RAF, could not maintain cover, though one got a U-boat on the 20th. As the ships drew closer to Newfoundland the intermittent fog that had helped and hindered both U-boats and convoys became total. Now they were within Liberator range of Gander and the first aircraft took off at 02:30 on the 22nd, but when they reached the convoy the fog was still impenetrable. All day relays of Liberators stuck with the convoy, though even at 100 feet (30 m) the surface was still invisible. At 15:30 the fog finally rolled away and within minutes the men of 10 (BR), the finest airmen to fly the Northwest Atlantic, were in position and attacking. Both the merchant seamen and the navy were astounded to see "the air was filled with Liberators" – "not 'on the way' or 'expected in two hours' but actually flying around the convoy."

First into action was W/O J Billings in 597 L who sighted U-270 and attacked through heavy flak which knocked out an engine and wounded the navigator. Four accurate depth charges deluged U-270 with water and then a fierce gun battle ensued. U-270 did not dive and so Billings could not use his remaining warload – a pair of acoustic torpedoes. **

F/L Martin (3rd from right, back row) and crew beside Liberator 595 X in January of 1944. The two sub silhouettes commemorate this crew's 2 engagements (in one sortie) of the previous September. The aircraft's capacious bomb bay was loaded with 2 of the then new-technology, top secret Proctor acoustic homing torpedoes plus 6 depth charges and an auxiliary fuel tank (port forward rack) at the time of the attacks. Having expended all of this ordnance in the first attack, the second sub was engaged with gunfire only, though with some success. The buoy / marker launch chute fairing, unique to GR/ASW Liberators, can be seen under the centre-rear fuselage, just beyond the starboard main landing gear tire, in the photo opposite.

this photo: LAC NA-A277

opposite photo: LAC PL21759

Finally, Billings abandoned the contest as fuel ran low and U-270 limped back to France on the surface with a badly damaged pressure hull. During the battle Billings had called for assistance but F/L JR Martin in 595 X replied "I have a UB of my own on my hands." This was U-377 and 595's battle was similar to 597's – four depth charges which damaged but did not sink and a gunnery duel in which the U-boat's skipper was badly wounded. Martin was able to drop his two "Zombies" after U-377 submerged but neither of the temperamental weapons scored. U-377 made it back to port, obtaining medical assistance from another U-boat en route. Immediately after U-377's disappearance, Martin engaged in another gunnery duel, this time with U-402, until the latter escaped in a fogbank. The Liberator stayed in radar contact with the sub, and stayed between it and the convoy. Just after nightfall F/O A Cirko in 600 N located and engaged U-275 in a gun battle, but did not attack with d/c's as permission to drop the necessary flares was denied by the naval escort for fear they would illuminate the convoy. U-275 had been forced down, but, as 10 (BR) had

only been able to intervene in the last hours of the 22nd, enough U-boats were close enough to mount a final attack on the convoy that night. Next morning, before dawn, F/L JF Green in 594 P engaged one briefly in the minimal visibility. The U-boats were forced to stay submerged most of the day, but six hours later Green caught U-422 on the surface and made a d/c attack, gunnery attack and a follow-up with two Zombies. At dusk F/L Ingrams in 596 Y also caught U-422 on the surface, but the attack was spoiled by an accidental premature release of the d/c's. In both attacks U-422 suffered gunfire casualties and damage to the upper deck. This ended the battle – a bizarre two-day conflict in poor visibility with U-boats and Liberators dodging in and out of fogbanks until, finally, the U-boats had no hope of getting into attacking position. This was 10 (BR)'s big hour though not its last encounter for the year. On 26 October F/L RM Aldwinkle in 586 A was credited with the sinking of a U-boat, presumably U-420. Recently, in some quarters, this has been reassessed as an error, with U-420's loss attributed to "unknown causes." However, an examination

of the photos of the attack, with an immense eruption of oil and water towering over the depth charge plume renders this "reassessment" exceedingly dubious.

After the defeat of the wolfpacks in the fall of '43, U-boats, by now schnorkel-equipped, only entered 10 (BR)'s operational area singly or in small groups as the hide-and-seek era of modern ASW had commenced. Few U-boats were sunk – 10 (BR) had some encounters, though no kills – but the subs achieved little. Despite GR.VI's coming on strength, the aircrew preferred the GR.V (Can) some of which were now fitted with Leigh Lights and retractable rocket rails. After VE Day 10 (BR) moved to Torbay near St. John's where it was disbanded in August 1945. There was one final tragedy. One of the Liberator's serious faults was that it could not be ditched successfully – no more than a handful from all nations and services ever accomplished this. On 6 July 1945 595 X was forced down off the Newfoundland coast and the pilot, F/O FD Gillis did the impossible, dying himself, but saving his crew, who got out in the dinghy.

Supermarine
Stranraer
Maritime Patrol Aircraft

The Supermarine Stranraer, a big twin-engined biplane flying boat, and a photogenic aircraft if ever there was one, seems to be nearly synonymous with the early WWII days of the RCAF. Nevertheless, its career has a faint air of anti-climax. While sturdy and reliable it was not initially available in expected quantities, had departed EAC just as the U-boats were arriving and, for an embarrassingly lengthy period, was a WAC mainstay guarding against an enemy who might come – but didn't.

The Stranraer represented the end of a long line of twin-engined biplane flying boats that had served the RAF well in the years between the wars. A successor to the Supermarine Southampton and Scapa, the prototype flew in 1935 and the first of 17 production examples entered service in 1936, finally leaving the squadrons in 1940. It was of metal construction, except for fabric-covered wings and tail units, and powered by Bristol Pegasus X or XXII engines. It normally carried a crew of five. While the cabin was enclosed and featured cooking and sleeping facilities, the nose, midships and tail gunners' positions were usually wide open.

When the RCAF was choosing a long range general reconnaissance aircraft the Stranraer was an obvious choice, given the then policy of adopting RAF types. Canadian Vickers was an equally obvious choice of manufacturer with its aircraft and ship building background. A contract for three Stranraers was placed in November 1936 and successive contracts brought the total to 40. Serial numbers allotted were 907-16, 918-23, 927-38 and 946-57. Despite being by far the largest and most complex aircraft to be built in Canada to that time, construction went smoothly and 907 first flew in October 1938. It was delivered to 5 (GR) – later 5 (BR) – at Dartmouth, Nova Scotia, the next month. Eight had been delivered by the start of the war plus two more by November. Eight had gone to 5 (BR) and the other two to 4 (BR) in Western Air Command. At this point the Stranraer production story plunges headlong into murkiness as the next of the remaining thirty did not come off the line

This photo of Stranraer 955 offers a rare full-colour glimpse of the 4-colour countershaded Temperate Sea Scheme that was unique to maritime-use biplanes. The photo also shows the beaching gear, mooring drogues (hanging over the sides, mid-fuselage), boarding "stairs" and upper wing servicing ladder. Pat Bay, circa 1942.

for almost a year – late October 1940. The last was taken on RCAF charge in November 1941. Canadian Vickers blamed slow delivery of parts, particularly from England, the RCAF blamed the company's conflicting priorities and incompetence in running a production line, while there seems to have been delay in finalizing the contracts. [Hopefully, further research will illuminate this matter. However, the bottom line is that the small Stranraer force with which the RCAF entered the war did not increase for nearly a year.]

By September 1939, 5 (BR) was well-worked up on the type and commenced operations at once – primarily convoy escorts and patrols. In an emergency they would also have provided navigation for EAC's sole striking force, 10 (BR)'s antediluvian Wapitis. The winter of 1939-40 was a tough one and it was then that EAC came face to face with the unpalatable fact that flying boats, particularly partially open biplanes, simply were not suitable for winter operations in the western North Atlantic. Floating ice was a hazard and the aircraft could not be left in the water as the hulls would ice up. The Stranraer's bomb carriers were so near the water that they could also freeze up, while the towering

superstructure was vulnerable to icing and headwinds and the open gun positions were completely uninhabitable. The squadron did its best with long-range tanks and enclosed bomb-cells but it was probably at this time that the RCAF really started to go off of flying boats. 5 (BR) soldiered through another winter, during which a trickle of new Stranraers arrived. In June 1941 the squadron thankfully started to train on Catalinas [see p.4], only to have them whipped away and given to 116 (BR). Finally, in the fall of 1941, because of the imminent arrival of Cansos and Canso A's and the unsuitability of the Stranraer, 5 (BR) was ordered before re-equipping to ferry its aircraft and those of the recently formed (and recently disbanded) 117 (BR) across country to WAC which was now to operate all Stranraers. Here the Stranraers fully or partially equipped 4, 6, 7, 9 and 120 (BR) as well as 13 (OT) and 166 (Comm) Squadrons and 3 OTU. There, off the spectacular BC coast, the aircraft gave reliable but unspectacular service – marred only by the embarrassment of the crews when operating beside USN squadrons with more modern equipment – until most were withdrawn from service in late 1944. A number went on to lead useful civilian lives while one still survives in beautiful condition in the RAF Museum.

Like all Canadian production Stranraers, 916 came off the Canadian Vickers line in an overall aluminum lacquer with a protective coat of clear marine varnish over the water contact areas of the hull and floats. As the nation went to a war footing, such finishes were progressively phased out in favour of multi-coloured camouflage paint schemes deemed more suitable to the aircraft's primary operational environment. For the most part, the RCAF adopted such wartime paint schemes from the RAF. In the Stranraer's case that meant a change to the special version of the Temperate Sea Scheme particular to biplane flying boats. Originated to lessen the contrast of the shadow areas of biplanes, it comprised Dark Slate Grey and Extra Dark Sea Grey upper surfaces with the countershaded areas — including the upper surfaces of the lower wings and the lower portion of the fuselage sides — correspondingly Light Slate Grey and Dark Sea Grey. All under surfaces were Sky. Fuselage markings — 3 letter codes, Type A roundels and serials — were usually placed in a similar manner to those on RAF Coastal Command Stranraers. The large Type B roundels on the upper wing tips and full coverage Type A fin flashes were retained while the underwing serials and Type A roundels of the factory scheme were removed. Although 9 (BR) was based much further north at Bella Bella, the 5.5 ton (empty) 916 is seen in the photograph being moved by the Patricia Bay Brute crane on the south coast of Vancouver Island.

It is interesting to note that although a performance-altering change in powerplant is often enough to warrant a change in the official Mark designation, Canada's Pegasus X engined machines (907-916 and 918-923) were never distinguished from their Pegasus XXII powered stablemates (927-938 and 946-957) in this manner. Our profiled aircraft is one of the earlier machines featuring 4 bladed wooden propellers (actually 2x 2-bladed units bolted together 90 degrees apart) whereas the later 955 in the photo at left uses more modern 2-position 3-bladed all metal deHavilland units. The RCAF Stranraer fleet had its defensive armament progressively upgraded. Entering service with Lewis .303s in all three positions, these were replaced, rather quickly it seems, by .30 Vickers VGO guns, which were in turn supplanted by .30 Browning M2s. Various combinations of the latter two guns on the same aircraft show up frequently in photographs, with the more effective Browning often occupying the nose and tail stations. The final arrangement was single Brownings in the nose and tail with a twin Browning amidships. The illustration depicts a Browning in the tail, a Vickers in the middle and, as is often seen, no gun or ring mount in the nose position. 250lb Mk.IV A/S bombs occupy the inner underwing hardpoints. The fairing at the strut-to-nacelle junction and single centreline mid-fuselage strut came late in the type's evolution. The slight nose-down cruise attitude and waterline grime and wear were typical Stranraer traits.

Supermarine (Canadian Vickers built) Stranraer #916 as KA•A of 9 (BR) Sqn, Western Air Command, Bella Bella, British Columbia, summer 1942.

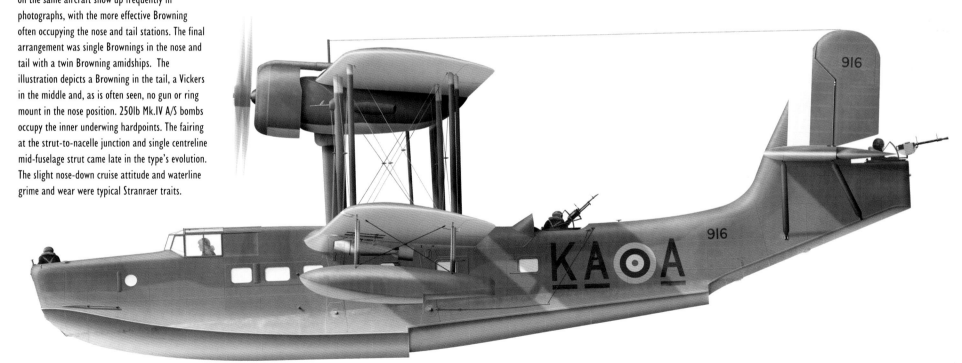

Bristol Bolingbroke IVW

General Reconnaissance Aircraft

On 27 October 1941 aircraft 9023 of 119 (BR) Squadron, RCAF Eastern Air Command, took off from Yarmouth, Nova Scotia. Although it was a routine navigation exercise, the aircraft carried a full war load – U-boats had started their first tentative sorties into North American waters. The crew was unaware both that 9023 was the last of the RCAF's 15 Bolingbroke IVW's to be delivered and that it was about to be the first to be written off. The exercise took the Bolingbroke over the Bay of Fundy, where it encountered foggy and hazy conditions. With darkness coming on the pilot, who was inexperienced and lacked confidence in his instrument flying ability, decided to divert to Dartmouth without informing Yarmouth (where the weather had cleared up). Over Digby the weather deteriorated further so, despite having more than three hours fuel remaining, he attempted a forced landing in St. Margaret's Bay. In the last stages of the descent the Bolingbroke hit a tree before it hit the water, so the landing was more precipitate than intended. Thanks to the help of nearby civilians (the RCAF knew nothing of the pilot's plight) all crew members made it to shore without serious injury. The aircraft was later salvaged, but proved a total write-off.

This episode possesses a measure of significance for two reasons. It is an indication of how starved for aircrew, particularly experienced men, the RCAF's Home War Establishment [HWE] squadrons were for the first years of the war. Despite the fact that the British Commonwealth Air Training Plan in Canada was now producing large numbers of trained aircrew, under this agreement only a very small number were allowed to go to the HWE. Hence, these units were chronically undermanned and new personnel, fresh from the training schools, had to acquire their skills on the job with minimal mentoring. Also, Bolingbroke 9023's demise was the swan song of the brief and not particularly brilliant operational career of that most obscure production variant of the Bolingbroke, the Mark IVW.

The fall of France and Britain's dangerous situation in June 1940 saw Canada's attitude to the war become increasingly urgent, not least in aircraft procurement. Only ten of the 18 Bolingbroke I's had been delivered and a further 12 "long-range Bolingbrokes" (later Mk.IV) were on order. The possibility of alternative power plants had already been under consideration, both for the general desirability of as much of any Canadian-built aircraft as possible being made in North America and in case of a potential disruption of supplies from Britain. By late June the preferred option was the Pratt and Whitney Twin Wasp Junior which, at 825 hp, was equivalent to the 800 hp Bristol Mercury VIII of the Bolingbroke I, but well under the 920 hp Mercury XV originally intended for the Bolingbroke IV. Space does not permit coverage of the decision-making process. Suffice it to say that, knowing a Bolingbroke IVW would have a tare weight 152 pounds (69 kg) greater than a Bolingbroke IV, but with only 90 per cent of the horsepower, the RCAF was well aware that with full long-range tanks and normal warload it would have an exceedingly poor power/weight ratio. Nevertheless, when, after a number of disappointments in procuring aircraft, it was decided on 30 July 1940 to increase the Bolingbroke IV's on order to 80, all were intended to have the American engine, except for enough Mercury XV-powered examples to keep production going until redesign could be accomplished.

text continued on p.42

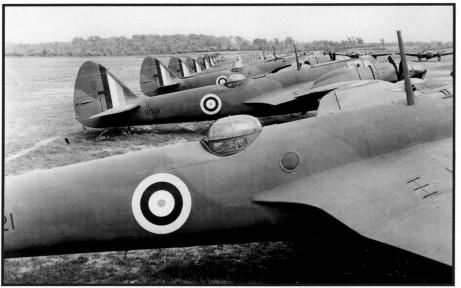

Not only does this pair of photos include almost all of the series production Bolingbroke IVWs ever built, but they also offer a fine study of this rare subtype, the unique features of which include the symmetrical humps over symmetrical nacelles, the shielded main landing gear covers, oddball Twin Wasp Junior engine cowlings, and clockwise-turning propellers. The Bristol Mk.II turret, wireless operator's "porthole", radio antenna mast, direction finder antenna "football" and overall finish are in common with its early-build Mercury-engined Mk.I and Mk.IV stablemates.

Bristol (Fairchild built) Bolingbroke Mk.IVW 9023 as DM•E of 119 (BR) Sqn, Eastern Air Command, Yarmouth, Nova Scotia, September-October 1941.

Like the Mercury-engined Bolingbroke IV 9066 on p. 20, 9023 was delivered in the same Dark Green and Dark Earth over Dark Night scheme but applied to the Bolingbroke IV manual's B pattern. Markings — both national and squadron level — were also identical to those on 9066 in size and colour. Standard defensive armament for all 15 Mk.IVWs was the antiquated Vickers drum-fed VGO .303. It is likely that, had the Twin Wasp powered Bolingbrokes seen the same extent of service life as the "straight IVs", their Bristol Mk.II turrets would have been upgraded to Mk.IIIA standard with the installation of twin belt-fed Browning .30cal M2 guns. A typical operational load for these underpowered maritime patrol aircraft comprised 2x 250lb anti-submarine bombs in the main bomb-bays plus various target markers and/or flares in the inner wing auxiliary ordnance bays, cabin stowage stations, and under-fuselage Light Series Stores Carriers. The latter could also be used for practice bombs as shown here. The clockwise-turning propellers, engines, engine cowls, and nacelle extensions (between wing leading edges and cowl flaps) are the main identifying aspects of this sub-variant of the Bolingbroke. Additionally, unlike the asymmetrical arrangement seen on Mercury-engined Mk.IVs, the IVWs featured identical "humps" above each wing nacelle (the nacelles themselves are symmetrical) and a low-slung twin exhaust arrangement that vented directly ahead of the landing gear (instead of above and to the side of it). The humps are due to the modified oil system. The left/right symmetry of the nacelles is due to the dinghy being moved from the rear port nacelle, where it was stowed in the Mark I, to the wing proper as in the Beaufort and Beaufighter. The Bolingbroke IV [see pp.20-24] retained the original larger port nacelle to accommodate the new oil system without having to provide a hump as in the smaller starboard nacelle. The new exhaust configuration called for the adding of side shields to the main landing gear covers to protect gear-leg-mounted hydraulic lines from becoming a fire hazard.

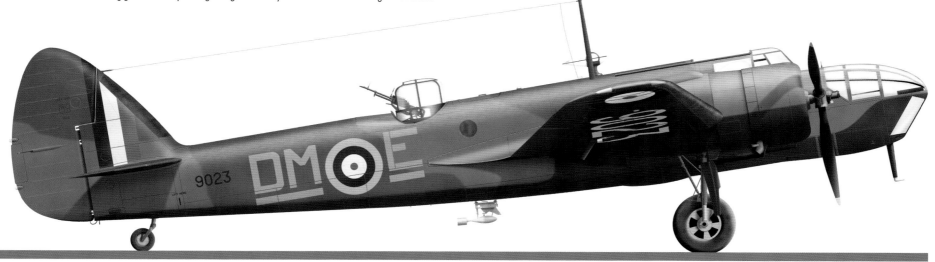

Acquiring the engines was not as simple as anticipated. The 250 in storage in Canada upon which the RCAF had counted were the property of the British, who refused to release them. Eventually 40 were obtained, complete with engine cowlings and exhaust manifolds from a cancelled French order with Chance Vought in the US, with an additional 25 from Mexico, where they had been fitted to ex-Spanish Bellanca 28-90's. The fifth Bolingbroke IV, 9005, became the prototype Mk.IVW, and flew in February 1941. Fourteen more (9010 to 9023) were produced in early 1941, all fitted with the ex-French engines. They were not delivered to the RCAF until July and August, as they had to wait for new runway construction at Fairchild before they could be flown out.

Twelve of the 15 Bolingbroke IVW's were issued to 119 (BR) Squadron in place of their Mark I's, most of which had been converted to fighters. Ten IVW's reached the squadron in the last two weeks of August. Unloaded they had the same performance below 10,000 feet (3000 m) as the Mk.I's, but were considerably noisier. With full load however, both 119 (BR) and the Test and Development Establishment at Rockcliffe found that the IVW's were incapable of maintaining altitude on one engine. Indeed, the Rockcliffe runways were too short for it to take off fully loaded with normal boost! Despite this, 119 (BR)'s IVW's were active through September and October with practice exercises, patrols and sub searches. To compensate for the low power the normal bomb load was reduced from 1000 (454 kg) to 500 pounds (227 kg).

In the meantime, Bolingbroke IV production was continuing with a steady supply of Mercury XV's coming along. Whether due to this fact, or to the IVW's poor performance, no more of this variant was built. Meanwhile, when in early October 1941 the RCAF was negotiating the Bolingbroke/ Hudson deal with Britain [see pp.23 and 60] it offered as a sweetener to transfer immediately 15 Bolingbrokes from EAC to Bombing and Gunnery (B&G) schools. Not surprisingly, on 4 November, just a week after 9023's ditching, 119 (BR) was ordered to ferry its IVW's, after only two months of operations, to 1 B&G and 6 B&G at Jarvis and Mountain View, Ontario, picking up Bolingbroke IV's at Fairchild on the way back. Little is yet known of the IVW's B&G School activities. However, it may be significant that most of the survivors were struck off strength in July 1944 – much earlier than other Bolingbrokes.

One Bolingbroke IVW that did achieve genuine distinction was 9010. Even now it is not widely known that Canada's National Research Council and the Massachusetts Institute of Technology on behalf of the US Government cooperated to develop airborne centimetric radar based on the British-developed magnetron. In January 1941 the RCAF agreed to send Boeing 247D 7655 (now fitted with a new nose and the Canadian portion of the radar) and a crew to Boston for airborne trials of the prototype AI-10 equipment. In June 1941 7655 was transferred to the RAF (subject to repayment) and shipped by sea to the UK. The radar went by air and was reinstalled in the Boeing – now RAF serial DZ203 – was further developed and installed in a Beaufighter. Bolingbroke IVW 9010 had been delivered initially to the Test and Development Establishment in Rockcliffe and was now selected as the second aircraft to go to Boston to assist in AI-10 development. Fitted with an unglazed moulded veneer nose it went to the US in the autumn of 1941 where the radar was successfully fitted. By March 1942 it was no longer required. It went back to Canada in the spring of 1942, was issued to EAC in June and spent the next ten months in tests and trials, particularly with submarines. It finished its operational career in the spring of 1943 training 10(BR) crews in the use of centimetric radar until their Liberators could be delivered. [see p.34]

With 119 (BR) Squadron's C/O, W/C NS MacGregor looking on, 9023 is recovered. This photo offers a good view of typical RCAF HWE underside markings and the Bolingbroke IVWs nacelle/cowl arrangement. Note also the extended landing/taxi lights and fuel dump pipes (near the "3" characters) under each wing, and cockpit bubble side windows — features that set all variants of the Bolingbroke Mk.IV apart from the earlier Mk.Is. Other items of note are the lugs for Light Series Stores Carrier attachment, the interruption in the port wing's de-icing boot to make way for the forward firing Browning .303 gun, and a live load of 2x 250lb A/S bombs in the port-side bomb bay. Early in the war this weapon, and its lighter 100lb counterpart, were the only ordnance available for smaller anti-submarine aircraft such as the Bolingbroke. The portly 450lb Mk.VII naval depth charge, originally adapted for external carriage on other aircraft, was much too rotund for its compact bomb bays. Later, as the smaller, more capable 250lb purpose-designed aircraft depth charges entered widespread service, the Bolingbroke was already on its way out of front line use in the Battle of the Atlantic.

Blackburn Shark II
Torpedo Bomber & Target Tug

January, 1942. Canada was at war with Japan and the RCAF, with its arc of Pacific seaplane bases – Ucluelet, Alliford Bay, Prince Rupert, Coal Harbour, Bella Bella - and their Stranraers and Sharks, as well as the isolated army detachments and AA batteries, plus the handful of naval warships and patrol vessels, were all watching for strange ships and aircraft. The Japanese failed to oblige, but some strange – or at least oddly-painted -aircraft did appear, a trio of seaplanes in a bizarre colour scheme of yellow, black and silver, roaring up and down the mountains, inlets and islands of the British Columbia coast. The RCAF's first Blackburn Sharks had found a new *raison d'être*.

The Shark, which had first flown in 1933, was the last of a series of Blackburn torpedo biplanes that had flown from RN carriers since 1918. Immensely strong with Warren Truss pattern interplane struts, it had numerous virtues, but was damned from birth by its engine, the Armstrong-Siddeley Tiger. This 14-cylinder, twin-row radial, was capable of a very smooth performance when it wished – which was seldom. Although Blackburn had pleaded with the Air Ministry to be allowed to build the Shark with something more reliable up front, they were refused. All but one of the 238 Sharks built for the RN plus another six for Portugal were Tiger-powered. After brief service with three carrier squadrons and a catapult flight the Sharks were withdrawn from active service in early 1938 and spent the rest of their career on second line tasks. Their only known contact with the enemy was a handful at Singapore that flew against the Japanese in January 1942.

By late 1935 the RCAF had made progress in its transition to a military air arm and the defence of Canada's coastline was an obvious priority. Patrol aircraft such as the Stranraer [see p.38] would be backed up by a squadron of torpedo bombers on each coast capable of operating from land or water. On the recommendation of the Air Ministry, at this time apparently oblivious to the Tiger's troubles, the Shark was chosen and a total of seven standard Shark II's, serials 501 to 507, were ordered for delivery in 1936/37. On arrival they were issued to the newly formed 6 (Torpedo Bomber)

Squadron at Trenton on Lake Ontario. For more than a year 6 (TB) was to grapple with the problem of becoming operational on a modern water-based torpedo bomber with a chronically unreliable engine. At one point the Sharks were ordered not to fly outside gliding distance of a suitable landing site! Bearings, crankcases and oil coolers were only some of the problem areas. Shark 504 was also employed to test a ski installation and an RCAF designed cockpit hood. The latter was not adopted as a Blackburn designed type was available. In 1938 all the RCAF Shark II's were withdrawn at intervals to be upgraded with new engine mounts and oil systems as well as an additional tail strut. Later in their service they received a three-bladed propeller and a massive Marston oil cooler.

In the meantime another 19 Sharks were ordered – two from Blackburn and 17 from Boeing Canada in Vancouver. These were designated Shark III (Canada) and powered by the Bristol Pegasus IX. Most of the RCAF's new service aircraft had Bristol engines and, as the RCAF commented on the lessons learned from the Tiger, "Canada cannot afford to adopt a motor that may require in-service development."

6 (TB) moved with five of the Shark II's to Jericho Beach, Vancouver, BC, in November 1938 and started working up as an operational squadron in 1939, making its first torpedo drops that summer. By now, the Tiger had become a moderately reliable motor, which was fortunate. During the first weeks of the war the first three Boeing-built Shark III's plus a Shark II were written off while taking off or landing in heavy swells. The squadron, which was now redesignated Bomber Reconnaissance, carried on for a few months with four Shark II's and a British-built Shark III in two detachments, three Sharks at Jericho Beach and two at Ucluelet, on the west coast of Vancouver Island – Canada's entire Pacific air striking force! By the end of 1939 the Shark III's which, despite initial misfortune, were strong, reliable aircraft, were being delivered and issued to 6 (BR) and, later, 4 (BR). The Shark II's, now a non-standard minority, became available for other tasks. 6 (BR) became partly responsible for the landplane training of 119 (BR), a "non-permanent" squadron that had been activated in September

Shark II 504 was refitted with wheeled undercarriage in February 1940. At the same time the opportunity was taken to apply the code letters. Considering that it was designed as a single-engined shipborne aircraft, the Shark is surprisingly large (note the crewman in the cockpit). The type's inherent sturdiness, exemplified by its massive main landing gear and wing struts, is strikingly evident in this photograph. Other details, such as the automatic aerodynamically-operated slats in their normal non-flying extended position on the upper wing's leading edge, and port-side boarding stirrup are also visible in this view. The odd-shaped bump through the E code letter is the housing for the torpedo depth setting gear. Below it the aircraft carrier catapult pick-up points, and to the rear of those the arrester hook attachment structure are remnants of the type's carrier-borne design. Neither were put to use in RCAF service.

1939. In order to provide training on military landplanes, Sharks 503 and 504 were re-equipped with wheels in February 1940 and spent a month with 119 at Sea Island. Later that spring, three Shark II's went to 4 (BR) until its Shark III's were all delivered. Then, in early May 1940, both Shark squadrons moved with their Shark III's to their wartime stations – 4 (BR) to the RCAF seaplane base at Ucluelet and 6 (BR) to that at Alliford Bay in the Queen Charlotte Islands. The story of these squadrons and of 7 (BR), which took over the Shark III's in December 1941 and operated them until September 1943, is much too large to be covered here.[An Aviaeology monograph on the Shark is in preparation—ed.]

The five surviving Shark II's (505 had crashed before leaving Trenton and 507 in September 1939) were about to enter the last, and possibly most useful, stage of their career. 501 and 503 were issued to 111 (CAC) at Patricia Bay, which was suffering a temporary dearth of service aircraft after its Lysanders had been shipped overseas, and worked very hard from July to October 1940, when they were turned in. By this time WAC had started to expand with the arrival of the Stranraers and Deltas [see pp.25 and 38]. However, all of these were water-based – BC's terrain was rivalled in scenic grandeur only by its lack of airfield sites. To provide gunnery practice for the BR squadrons and local naval and military units, Shark II's 502 (recently returned from the East), 504

and 506 were converted to target tugs and issued to 122 (Composite) Squadron at Pat Bay in December 1941. In an unusual version of the TT colour scheme, where the stripes formed a chevron rather than a diagonal, this gaudy trio – 502 with a wind-driven winch, 504 and 506 with electric ones – flew nearly non-stop all around the BC coast in all kinds of weather. 506 crashed on 18 June 1942 but the other two carried on, supplemented in the last months of 1943 by a few Shark III's. Meanwhile, in April 1942, Shark II's 501 and 503 were also converted to target tugs and, clad in modest grey, issued to 7 (BR) to fill the same role in the Prince Rupert area. At last, between November 1943 and July 1944, all RCAF Sharks, by now worked nearly to death and a maintenance headache, were scrapped, except for 502 and four III's, which were issued "under the counter" to five RN escort carriers for use in deck and hangar drills – probably the only Sharks to embark on a carrier for five years!*

Blackburn Shark II 504 as XE•C of 6 (BR) Sqn, Western Air Command, Sea Island, British Columbia, February-March, 1940.

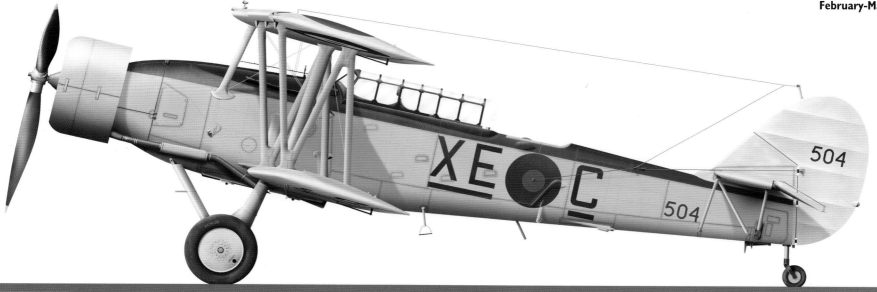

Shark II 504 was one of the original 7 aircraft built by Blackburn under contract number 455279/35. It is painted in the original Shark scheme – Light Grey fuselage and struts, black top decking, and doped Aluminum wing and tail surfaces. When 6 (BR) detached several aircraft to Sea Island (Vancouver) to assist in the training of newly arrived 119 Squadron aircrew, one of these was Shark 504, which arrived on 23 February. It remained active at Sea Island until 14 March 1940 and, shortly thereafter (end of April), went into storage with 3 RD. Full 3 letter codes were applied to all 6 (BR) aircraft at this time, including the Sea Island detachment. The low-visibility Type B fuselage roundels seem to give the aircraft a more warlike appearance; although photos indicate that bomb racks were not installed, the torpedo sighting bars (black line between cabane struts above the nose) and the nose gun with sights were retained. The aircraft is fitted with the later-service three bladed Rotol Schwartz-coated wooden propeller in place of the original two-blader, and the triple-strut tail support; the latter a uniquely RCAF modification. The tailwheel is apparently a smaller unit than that originally installed, while a Marston oil cooler has yet to replace the factory original. Very early in its career 504 was used to test a Canadian-designed cockpit canopy as part of the type's winterization program. This was eventually abandoned in favour of the original Blackburn-designed arrangement seen here.

Shark II (Target Tug) 504 as a very colourful float-equipped machine in the hands of 122 (K) Squadron at Pat Bay. Although at first glance its paint scheme appears to be the standard one for target tugs— diagonal black stripes over yellow overall (see Lysander on p.54) — it is unusual in several respects. The black along the top fuselage was retained and even mirrored on its undersides, and carried up over the fixed horizontal tail surfaces. The remaining black diagonals would normally have been rendered in one direction, but on at least two of 122(K)s Sharks — 502 and 504 — it was "handed", sweeping rearward from outboard to inboard on all wing surfaces and rearward top to bottom on the fuselage sides. Presumably the floats should also have received the black over yellow paint, but they remained mostly unrefinished with the exception of uniformly black undersides. Having become a target tug in January 1942, 504 went into storage in February 1944 and was finally reduced to spares in April 1944. The photo may have been taken during maintenance as the pulley support frame is not present under the fuselage. The torpedo depth gear fairing, trailing aerial fairlead, and gunner's wind deflector have been removed while a new Marston oil cooler hangs below the nose to starboard, the older unit having been removed from underneath the starboard wing root.

Blackburn Shark II (Target Tug) 504 as AG-D of 122 (K) Sqn, Western Air Command, Patricia Bay, British Columbia, through 1942.

Supermarine
Spitfire FR.IX & FR.XIV
Reconnaissance Fighters

The fighter reconnaissance aircraft and its role was a product of rapid development during WWII, particularly in the RAF. Initially that service had forgotten the lessons learned in the last months of WW1 and relied on slow two-seaters such as the Lysander for all army cooperation duties. Bitter experience in 1940 forced a reassessment, which resulted in the task being handed over to fighter aircraft equipped with both guns and cameras. They operated in pairs, one to carry out the primary task and one to provide the observation, warning and protection previously the responsibility of the gunner. Tomahawks were rapidly superseded by Mustangs [see p.8] and by D-day techniques had advanced to previously undreamed of levels which were heightened by actually working with an army locked in battle. By this time attrition had taken a toll of the Mustangs and an increasing number of the FR squadrons had re-equipped with suitably modified Merlin-powered Spitfire IX's. These proved such a success that later no less than 430 of the 957 formidable Griffon-powered Mk XIV's were built as FR models.

Both 414 and 430 RCAF squadrons were still equipped with Mustang I's at the time of D-day. While 430 kept its Mustangs until it transitioned directly to Spit XIV's in December 1944, 414 had just converted to Spit IX's when it flew to France on 15 August. One of these was MJ351, S, normally flown by F/L Ken Lawson, who named the aircraft *Violet-Dorothy* after his mother and wife. *Violet-Dorothy* went into action immediately with a tactical reconnaissance flight over the Antwerp/Bergen op Zoom/Breda area on the 16th. Space prohibits a detailed description of subsequent operations but over the next six months MJ351 flew 120 operational sorties – 84 tactical reconnaissance, 18 photo, and 15 artillery shoots plus an area search, a photo confirmation and a contact reconnaissance – frequently encountering fire from the efficient German flak. Aerial opposition was rare – indeed the first was a mistaken attack by Spitfires on 10 February 1945. There was a running fight with four Me262's on 21 February with no damage on either side, while the pair of Spits were bounced by 20-plus FW190's on 9 March and had to fight their way out. *Violet-Dorothy's* wingman claimed a kill and one damaged. Her charmed life ended on 19 March 1945 when, on a photo op over Germany, engine trouble forced her down to 4000 feet (1200 m) – optimum height for light flak. Although his wingman dived to draw the flak, P/O WA Glaister, who was flying MJ351 that day instead of F/L Lawson, had to bail out. He was taken prisoner but four weeks later turned up at the squadron, having escaped.

F/L Lawson had flown 25 of his 68 missions up to that point in MJ351. There was a second FR.IX *Violet-Dorothy*, but little information is available as to her true identity. After reviewing his logbook for us, Ken Lawson suggests that it may have been either ML268 or MJ930. Of the 24 missions he flew in the 21 days between the loss of *Violet-Dorothy* and his first sortie on the squadron's new FR.XIVEs, four each were logged in ML268 and MJ930; more than in any other post-MJ351 Mk.IX. Whichever the case, her career was necessarily brief due to 414's re-equipment. The third and final *Violet-Dorothy* was MV348, one of the new Spit XIV's that were reaching the squadron in April. It flew its first operation on 24 April, the first of eleven (including three on 3 May – tactical recces over Lubeck, Bremen and Kiel). In logging 23 FR.XIV sorties, Lawson was at MV348's controls for nine of those. He and *Violet-Dorothy* were active to the end.

Above: *Violet-Dorothy* was a Merlin-engined Spitfire Mk.IX especially modified with camera controls, a camera heating system, and camera mounts for the demanding fighter reconnaissance (FR) role.

photo: LAC AC651

Left: Later on, the manufacturer turned out ready-made FR Spitfires based on the longer-nosed Griffon-engined Mk.XIV. The new-build FRs identified as 414 Squadron aircraft featured the rear vision canopy while those in service with the RCAF's 430 Squadron were of the normal canopied variety and most likely FRU conversions using the same recce-associated components as the Mk.IXs.

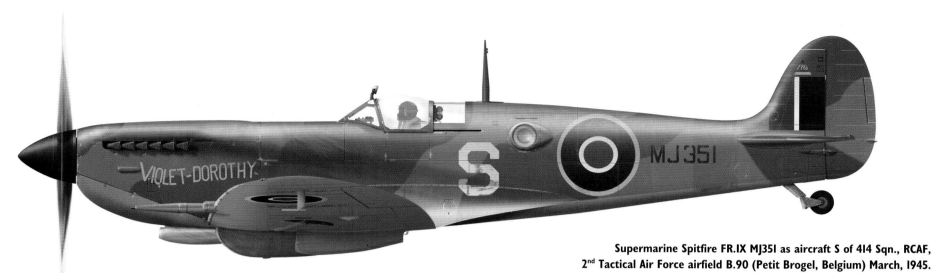

Supermarine Spitfire FR.IX MJ351 as aircraft S of 414 Sqn., RCAF, 2nd Tactical Air Force airfield B.90 (Petit Brogel, Belgium) March, 1945.

Spitfire FR.IX MJ351 started out as an LF.IXC (low-altitude optimised pure fighter variant) produced by Vickers-Armstrong at Castle Bromwich approximately mid-to-late 1943. After a time in pre-service limbo with 39 Maintenance Unit, it was issued to 340 (Ile-de-France) Squadron where it was used on operations from about February of 1944. Later in the year MJ351 was in the hands of 84 Group Service Unit who apparently sent it to the Forward Repair Unit (FRU — formerly 511 FRU) for "major repair." This was most certainly the FR conversion work, after which MJ351 went directly to 414 Squadron as an FR.IX (see text, p.46). The FRU's triangular emblem appears on both sides of the upper fin on all reference photos of 414's converted Spitfire IXs seen to date. A 45 or 90 (shown) gallon drop tank could be slung under the belly. Both fighter-recce squadrons — 414 and 430 — within 39 Wing used specialized FRU-converted Spitfires after a long period on the earlier Mustang I [see p.8].

MV348 was factory-built as an FR aircraft by Supermarine Aviation (Vickers) at Southampton against one of the first contracts for the Griffon-engined Mk.XIV. In fact, this particular aircraft was a production prototype for what was known as the interim configuration fighter-recce sub-type at Southampton. After completion it went to 39 MU before being issued to 414 Squadron in April of 1945. In profile view the most readily apparent changes due to the Griffon engine were the longer, declined thrust-line nose with its massive 5 bladed prop and the larger vertical tail. Although the bubble canopy is most often associated with the fighter-recce Mk.XIVs, both fighter and fighter-recce sub-types existed with the standard canopy (as seen on the Mk.IX above). The particular exhaust stack design illustrated is believed to be associated with early-production, low-level optimized Griffon 65 engines. In August of 1945 MV348 suffered a category AC accident. Since 414 had disbanded by then, this may have occurred in the hands of a new operator —either 2 Squadron or 123 Wing RAF HQ flight. If so, the retention of F/L Lawson's personal marking and the "S" aircraft-in-squadron code is noteworthy. The lower rudder repair evident in the photo may be as a result of this incident. The paint scheme on both of these Spitfires is the typical Day Fighter Scheme of the era — Ocean Grey and Dark Green upper surfaces with Medium Sea Grey undersides. A factory applied rear fuselage Sky band was oversprayed in the adjacent camouflage colours while the similarly coloured spinner was overpainted matte black (Night). Extensive weathering and finish touch-up were the norm for these highly utilized tactical recce machines.

Supermarine Spitfire FR.XIVE MV348 as aircraft S of 414 Sqn., RCAF, 2nd Tactical Air Force airfield B.154 (Soltau, Germany), 28 April - 6 May, 1945.

Bristol **Beaufighter** TF.X
Maritime Strike Fighter

Of all the fighter aircraft of WWII the Bristol Beaufighter stands supreme for an appearance of brutal and menacing force. With its sturdy but streamlined fuselage tucked between the two massive engines it gives the impression of a champion heavyweight boxer. It was undeniably an effective and versatile warplane, first as a night fighter – a role in which among other units it was employed by 406, 409 and 410 Squadrons RCAF and 125 (Newfoundland) Squadron RAF [This last unit will be covered in a future AviaDossier]. The Beau also served with distinction over the Mediterranean and North Africa, in Southeast Asia and with the RAAF and USAAF. Arguably its most effective and certainly most visibly spectacular service was as a strike fighter with RAF Coastal Command. An attack by an RAF Strike Wing was an unbelievably awesome episode. The blast of sound from the Hercules engines and the multiple cannons of the fighters and flak, the incandescent tracer, the rocket trails and the explosions and myriad splashes and plumes of water – all in a matter of seconds – was an experience that few forgot and, frequently, few survived. It was never one-sided – in the last years of WWII comparatively small German ships carried flak batteries greater than those of major warships in 1939 – while the Beau, neither particularly fast nor manoeuvrable, was normally no match for a single-engined fighter.

The Bristol Beaufighter was the most successful result of all the attempts to develop an effective warplane from the design concepts that had produced the Blenheim I, Bolingbroke [see pp. 20 and 40], Blenheim IV and Beaufort. Conceived in late 1938 to meet a requirement for a heavy twin-engined fighter, it was based on the Beaufort torpedo bomber with a new fuselage, more powerful Bristol Hercules engines, and half the crew (two instead of four). It carried a very heavy armament of four 20 mm cannon and six .303 machine guns. The prototype flew in July 1939 and the first Beaus entered squadron service in September 1940. No less than 5,562 had been built in the UK when production ceased in September 1945. Besides the Mk.I they included the Merlin-engined Mk.II, the Mk VI with the more powerful Hercules and the most numerous version, the TF.X [Torpedo Fighter, Mark Ten] strike fighter for Coastal Command, of which 2205 were produced. The TF.X had the same engines as the Mk.VI, modified for maximum output at lower altitudes, with provision for a torpedo under the fuselage or rails for eight rockets under the wings as well as navigation equipment more suited to maritime operations.

The Canadian unit destined to acquire fame as probably the most proficient practitioners of the art of Beaufighter strikes was the first of the RCAF's six overseas WWII maritime squadrons – 404 "Buffalo" Squadron. It was formed on 15 April 1941 at Thorney Island as a coastal fighter unit with Blenheim IVF's – essentially a Blenheim IV light bomber with four .303 machine guns in an under-fuselage pack. 404 commenced operations in September 1941 from Dyce near Aberdeen, where its first enemy was the consistently bad Scottish weather. This continued when the unit moved to Sumburgh in the

text continued on p.50

These two photos illustrate LZ451 in the markings of 404's commander, W/C AK Gatward — and the changes in Coastal Command's markings — through the eventful summer of 1944. That above was taken very early in June shortly after the order came down to apply prominent black and white ID stripes to all Allied Expeditionary Air Force (AEAF) aircraft slated for operations on D-Day. Within the month, 404 moved from 19 to 16 Group and reverted to the old EE squadron code of its Blenheim days as seen below. Note that by this time the cockpit roof hatch has been replaced by one incorporating a rear view mirror, most probably scavenged from an earlier Mk.VI airframe, and, as evidenced by the dipole antenna now present under the tailplane, the aircraft has been upgraded by the addition of a radio altimeter system. Communications gear, never a shortcoming on the Beaufighter, has also been upgraded, as indicated by the tall whip aerial just behind the pilot's cockpit. The deliberately angled settings of the Mk.IB Rocket Projectors (rails) show up well in this view, as do the liberal patches of red doping around the cannon ports, AEAF stripes overpainted onto the clear landing light covers (port wing, just above the outer pair of rockets) and Gatward's unique nose art. Though undeniably marked as the commander's mount, LZ451 was often flown by other pilots on many of the unit's more notable missions. While in the markings shown below, for example, on 21 July 1944 it was flown by S/L Shoales who led a strike against enemy shipping off the Frisian Islands that resulted in the sinking of a merchant vessel and a minesweeper. The aircraft suffered fire damage, and the navigator burn injuries, but they made it back to base. It could take punishment as well as dish it out. *Upper Photo: John Melson col.*   *Lower Photo: LAC PA145680*

Bristol Beaufighter TF.X LZ451 as 2•M of 404 Sqn., RCAF, RAF Coastal Command, Davidstow Moor, circa late June 1944.

Operational with 404 Squadron since approximately September / October of 1943, LZ451 was one of the first batch of 480 Beaufighters built to full TF.X (Torpedo Fighter, Mark Ten) specification at the Bristol Aeroplane Company's busy Old Mixton MAP (Ministry of Aircraft Production) shadow factory. Prior to this, 404 had been operating interim coastal strike fighter Mk.XIC's. The revised (from July of 1943) MAP paint specification for Coastal strike aircraft called for a single colour — Extra Dark Sea Grey — upper camouflage in place of the earlier Dark Slate Grey / Extra Dark Sea Grey disruptive pattern. The Sky undersides remained unchanged. While in the above markings, for a time LZ451's port prop hub was either light grey or dull metal while that opposite was dark grey or black. The overall finish on Strike Wing Beaus usually became patchy and faded during periods of intensive service and spot refinishing, with some upper areas looking more like the lighter Dark Sea Grey. The illustration above depicts a load of rockets with the 60lb high-explosive heads typical of those used on earlier Beaufighter anti-shipping missions, whereas those shown below feature 25lb solid-shot armour-piercing heads. The former were standard R/P ordnance on anti-flak Beaus. The latter were eventually settled on as the most effective for maritime strike aircraft; getting at least one or two AP rounds to puncture the hull below the waterline was much easier than hitting pinpoint targets on deck. Note the varied angles of the rails; the inboard and outboard pair are parallel to each other while the middle pair are offset at approximately 1 and 2 degrees [also see p.48 photo]. As anti-shipping tactics evolved, Beau strike groups would include a mix of aircraft armed with both rocket types (whereas Coastal's ASW specialist units stuck to the AP version only). Note that the rockets are illustrated as plugged in on the in flight profile while left unplugged on the parked profile. As a safety precaution, rockets were usually made live only just before take-off. Although LZ451 was built as a Torbeau, the torpedo gear and crutches had been removed as the squadron relied on rockets in its anti-shipping missions. Oddly, two other reference photos of 2 • M show a pair of Universal Bomb Carriers under the forward fuselage — even with a full load of rockets present — indicating that 404 used bombs as well. However, it is highly unlikely that both types of ordnance were carried simultaneously in a single sortie.

Bristol Beaufighter TF.X LZ451 as EE•M of 404 Sqn., RCAF, RAF Coastal Command, Strubby, July -September 1944.

Shetlands in late October. For almost a year this, with periods at Dyce, was to be 404's home whence the Blenheims carried out patrols and shipping escorts as well as covering Coastal Command offensive operations off the Norwegian coast. While 404's Blenheims gave a surprisingly good account of themselves on the few occasions they encountered enemy aircraft, they were still grossly inferior to German fighters, and the Canadians repeatedly requested re-equipment. Despite promises, this did not occur until September 1942, when the first Beaufighters arrived. They were Mk.II's with Merlin engines – faster but less stable than the Mk.I's. In late January 1943, 404 moved to Chivenor in Devon to provide cover for Coastal's anti-submarine effort over the Bay of Biscay. The squadron's first Beaufighter successes were on 23 March when it accounted for two Ju88 long range fighters. Soon after this, 404 returned to Scotland, first to Tain and then to Wick in the extreme northeast of Scotland, where it would remain for a year.

In the meantime, Coastal Command, realizing that the Hudson bombers and Beaufort and Hampden torpedo bombers equipping its strike squadrons were too slow and vulnerable, while the Mosquitoes it coveted would not be allotted in significant numbers for some time, decided to standardize on the Beaufighter. The first of this type

modified to carry torpedoes, known familiarly as Torbeaus, reached Coastal in the summer of 1942, and the first experimental strike wing comprising a squadron of Torbeaus and another of escort and anti-flak Beaufighters was formed in November. 404 Squadron at Wick, now re-equipped with Beaufighter XIC's and part of 18 Group, would play a leading role in developing both strike-wing tactics and the use of rocket projectiles [RP]. In the beginning, however, it flew escort and anti-flak missions for Torbeaus and Hampdens. In July detachments began to operate from Sumburgh as escorts to R/P armed Beaus of 235 Squadron, RAF. It was at this time that it first became apparent to the observant 404 men that the 60-pound (27 kg) explosive heads on the R/P damaged but failed to sink the enemy vessels. Another squadron activity was covering naval forces and it was on one of these operations, on 28 July, that 404 Beaufighters shot down four BV138 flying boats.

In August 1943 operations from Sumburgh ceased and 404 re-equipped with Beaufighter TF.X's – a version specifically tailored to Coastal's needs - and commenced R/P training. It was at this point that 404 really came into its own. Its sole RAF pilot, S/L AK Gatward (a colourful character, who in 1942 had flown a lone Beaufighter to Paris to drop a tricolour

text continued on p.52

LZ451 displaying yet another markings variation. By the time of their move north to join 18 Group in Scotland from 3 September 1944, many 404 Squadron aircraft still carried invasion stripes on the lower curvature of the fuselage, and quite possibly below the wings for a brief period. The former commander's aircraft is somewhat unusual in having its stripes remain wrapped around the fuselage. The squadron and aircraft-in-squadron codes were overpainted (manually, with brushes, by appearance) on the rear fuselage and reapplied in Sky (some sources state White) further forward, similar to those on other northern strike wing Beaufighters. Note the progressive fading of the main paintwork which, when combined with repaint patches, fuel spills and windshield de-icing over-spray appears to effectively create a new, albeit unofficial, multi-coloured camouflage scheme. The wing is devoid of projectors (rails), though the adapter pannier part of the R/P installation remains. This configuration was not unusual if the aircraft was to "ride shotgun" exclusively cannon armed.

Photo: Jimmy Forrester col.

Bristol Beaufighter TF.X LZ451 as EE•M of 404 Sqn., RCAF, RAF Coastal Command, Banff, Scotland, October 1944.

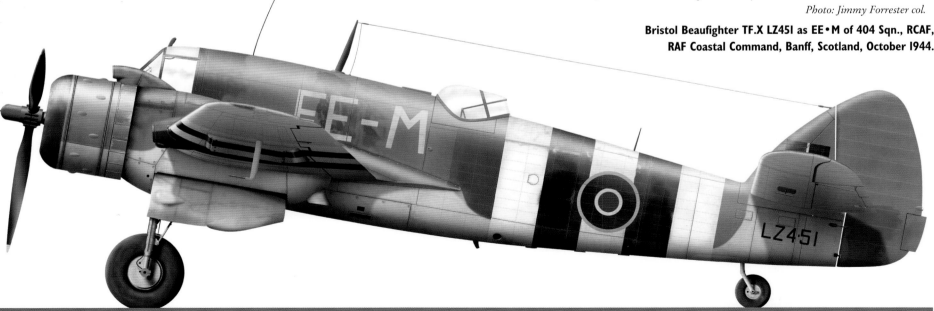

3 photo: LAC PL33496

2 photo: LAC PL33498

1 photo: LAC PL33499

4 photo: LAC C5274

Beau-fight! Clockwise from lower left:

1 & 2) Misty harbour, tortured water and a battered vessel mark this sequence as a German flak ship bears the full fury of a Beau strike. The smoke trails and impacts of rockets just launched from an aircraft on the opposite heading have yet to clear and already the strike camera catches this Beaufighter's rockets leaving the rails, as its cannon fire walks towards the vessel. Flak platforms elevated on towers above the deck and superstructure can be seen in at least 8 locations.

3) 12 August 1944 , a similar scene unfolds off La Pallice, over the *Sauerland*, a heavily-armed *sperrbrecher* as Beaufighters of 236 and 404 Squadrons out of Davidstow Moor leave the ship foundering, soon to be sunk by the Royal Navy. The aircraft directly above the target is reportedly that of W/C Gatward.

4) A trio of Coastal strike Beaufighters over icy waters within a Norwegian fjord.

This close-up of the nose of W/C Gatward's Beaufighter LZ451 EE•M late in its service (presumably while at Banff) shows the aircraft's unique markings in detail and a strike camera now installed in the nose tip. The difference indicated by the 6 yellow and the 8 red rocket/swastika symbols is not known, but these appear to have been left unchanged since at least August of 1944 (when the main photo on p.48 was taken). The Boxing Buffalo represents both the squadron's *Ready to Fight* motto and the Buffalo namesake. Behind it is W/C Gatward's rank pennant. W/C Pierce assumed command 24 August 1944 but it is not known if he flew this aircraft. *Photo: John Melson col.*

on the *Arc de Triomph*) was impressed by the R/P, but felt the 25 lb armour-piercing head was more effective than the 60 lb HE as a ship-sinker. Along with other 404 men, particularly F/O S Shulemson, Gatward developed R/P use and squadron tactics to a high degree. Eventually the squadron was organized in two 7-plane sections, each with four anti-flak (one with 60 lb HE rockets and three with just cannon) Beaus and three strike aircraft with eight 25 lb R/P harmonized with the cannon. Space prohibits greater description of tactical evolution and Coastal Command policy. Suffice it to say that 404 brought its proficiency to such a level that, whatever shifts Coastal Command policy took, the squadron was permitted to retain its tactics and 25 lb R/P to the end.

From October 1943, 404 teamed up with Torbeau squadron 144 as 18 Group's strike wing, mainly operating against German shipping en route to or from Norwegian ports with considerable success though with some losses, mainly to flak. On 26 January 1944, however, a force of twelve Beaufighters, six from each of 144 and 404, were intercepted by Bf109's. A 404 Beau had been shot down and a 144 machine was in danger when the strike leader, 404's F/O Shulemson turned back to engage the '109. In an unequal running battle Shulemson saved the 144 aircraft and escaped destruction himself. He subsequently received the DSO – a rare award for a Flying Officer.

This eventful period ended when the wing was transferred to Davidstow Moor to protect the right flank of Operation Overlord, the Normandy invasion, as part of 19 Group. All other Beaufighter squadrons were to operate with bombs, but, in tribute to their expertise, 404 and 144 continued with their rocket and cannon tactics. On 7 and 8 June they hit three German destroyers, 404 damaging two big *Narvik* class boats. Two of the three were finished off on 9 June by a force of RN and RCN destroyers. At the end of June, with few remaining targets, 404 went north to Strubby to attack shipping off the Dutch and German coasts, once again with considerable success. 404 still retained its R/P's, though most other squadrons had reverted to the torpedo. Some of these strikes were massive, such as one on the 21st with 45 Beaus against nine merchant ships and 21 escorts.

The Allied breakout in France in early August meant another transfer for 404 back to Davidstow Moor, where it operated against the German naval forces supporting the garrisons of the Biscay ports. 404's results were spectacular – in conjunction with 236, the only other R/P-Beau squadron, the Canadians sank six minesweepers, three *sperrbrechers* (merchant ships converted to escort vessels with tremendous flak capacity), two escort vessels and the destroyers *Z24* and *T24*.

With this job done, 404 moved back to Scotland, where in early September it became part of the Banff Wing and, in November, the Dallachy Wing operating against German shipping on the Norwegian coast. Many of the strikes involved night flights to a wing assembly point at first light off the target area – no mean navigational feat. In late 1944 and early 1945 enemy shipping hugged the Norwegian coast and took shelter there, while the *Luftwaffe* fighter force was strengthened. A combination of both led to "Black Friday" when the Dallachy Wing attacked a strong naval force inside a fjord supported by land-based flak and FW190's. The "Buffaloes" lost six Beaus with 11 of their 12 crewmen. The last 404 Beaufighter sorties were in March involving the distasteful task of attacking Norwegian lighthouses. The squadron then re-equipped with Mosquitoes and, in the last weeks of the war, flew long-range strikes over the Baltic.

Photos: LAC AC662 (above) & AC666

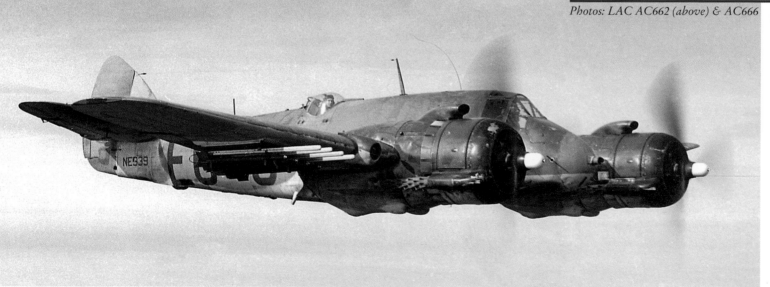

Beaufighter TF.X NE339 circa January 1945 when 404 Squadron was part of the Dallachy Strike Wing in Scotland. A year earlier, and marked as EE•U this aircraft was the mount of F/O Syd Shulemson when he drove off a Bf109G fighter and earned his DSO. Like many busy Beau crews of the period, Shulemson and Bassett had many other individual aircraft in their log books, for they flew whatever was available on the line when the mission came up. EO•U, even as EE•U, was not their usual mount. Sadly, on 24 March 1945 F/O Aljoe (pilot) and F/Sgt Orser (navigator) were lost with this aircraft during 404 Squadron's last Beaufighter strike. One other 404 crew was also lost in that action which cost the enemy two merchant vessels totalling just over 4,000 tons. The "Buffaloes" converted to Mosquito aircraft soon thereafter.

NE339 came from the second batch of Beaufighter TF.Xs built at Old Mixton and as such has features in common with LZ451 including the basic paint scheme, short spike antenna, and early Mk.VI style air intakes over the engine nacelles. On later TF.Xs these intakes were enlarged, extending forward over the cowls. Like LZ451, it also had the whip antenna and the extended strike camera lens fitted in the nose. Whether retrofitted or factory installed, the Mod 856 wingtips are also common to both aircraft. These replace the rear-facing wingtip formation light with a smaller pencil-shaped resin unit. With this modification the clear covers of the old fixture remain unchanged, but were frequently overpainted in the local finish colours, which often appear to have worn away. Note also that the R/P rails are set up differently. The inboard rail is set approximately parallel to the line of flight, the one next to it is declined about a half a degree, the one next to it another half degree and the outermost one is at least two degrees nose down. By early 1945 many 404 Beaus had changed to this lighter, less complex Mk.IIIA Rocket Projector (R/P rails) installation in place of the earlier Mk.IBs. The revised geometry of the arrangement may be indicative of the use of modified tactics or of later-production rocket motors which imparted different ballistic characteristics. Rocket warheads are of the 25lb AP type favoured for ship-busting. The larger photo opposite supports the notion that two wing guns may have been retained for sighting-in the heavier weapons. Unusual, as the normal Torbeau configuration did not include any wing guns at all. The torpedo carrying equipment is not present. The squadron code changed to EO in January of 1945 and the individual aircraft code U is repeated low on the nose cap. The left wing's landing light installation is protected by an ad hoc sheet metal cover. Close examination of the original photos reveals patchy overpainting on the mid and rear fuselage flanks where the earlier invasion stripes and EE•U codes had been. In a similar fashion to those on other early 1945 "up north" Coastal Command strike-fighter Beaus, the new codes were garishly large, often hand painted, and (apparently more often than not) hastily laid out resulting in varying degrees of uniformity of stroke and size from aircraft to aircraft and even character to character as seen here.

Westland Lysander III TT
Target Tug

The Westland Lysander, though never achieving fame or notoriety, saw considerable RCAF service during WWII. It was one of the types that got Canadian military aircraft production started and, in both Canadian and British-built versions, served with operational units and the BCATP for most of the war. It represented the final development of the classic army cooperation aircraft intended to work intimately with army units on artillery spotting and reconnaissance operations, entering service with the RAF in 1938. A total of 1,368 were built before UK production ceased in 1942. Despite their sturdy construction and near-STOL capabilities, Lysanders suffered severe losses in France in 1940 and though the type saw subsequent service in Greece, Africa, India and Burma, it was obvious that its designed role was a thing of the past. It did subsequently prove extremely useful in air-sea rescue, spy-dropping and pickup, and, significantly, as a target tug.

In 1938 the RCAF placed orders for 28 Lysanders – for some reason in three separate contracts for 12, 12 and 4 – to be built by National Steel Car at Malton, Ontario. These were Lysander II's with 905 horsepower Bristol Perseus II engines and were essentially similar to their British counterparts except for the use of larger metal skin panels. The first flew on 16 August 1939. Early Canadian Lysanders proved successful except for the inevitable deficiencies that plagued most British designs in Canada – inadequate oil coolers and cockpit heating, and fragile glazing – all of which were eventually rectified. Most of the first 28 Lysanders were issued to 2, 110 and 112 (Army Cooperation) Squadrons and 111 (Coast Artillery Cooperation) Squadron. 110 and 112 (AC), having absorbed 2 (AC), went overseas in 1940 where they operated RAF Lysanders (plus 6 RCAF ones) but saw no action until, renumbered as 400 and 402 Squadrons, they converted to Tomahawks and Hurricanes respectively.

In September 1940 the RCAF ordered another 96 Lysander II's, but reduced the order in December to 47, making a total of 75 of this mark. All (serials 416 to 490) had been delivered by April 1941. The majority were issued to the RCAF's six Coast Artillery Cooperation Detachments – Nos 1, 2, 3, 4, 5

and 6 at Saint John, NB, Dartmouth, NS, Patricia Bay, BC, Sydney, NS, Torbay, Newfoundland and Yarmouth, NS respectively. Their assigned role of cooperating with the shore defences should they engage an enemy warship was nominal – they were occupied mainly with radar calibration, search and rescue, and inshore patrols and sub searches. Indeed, one from 2 CAC Detachment carrying two 250 lb depth charges made a near-successful attack on U-96 on 23 February 1942, inflicting some damage.

In 1939 Britain had placed an order in Canada for 150 Lysanders, but by late 1940 this was redundant – Lysanders were no longer in high demand and UK production was sufficient. In order to keep the production lines open and because of a need in the BCATP for target tugs, the RCAF took over the order. These were Lysander IIIA's with Bristol Mercury XX's of 870 hp and were produced as target tugs designated III TT. All were completed in 1942 and serialed 2305 to 2454. Such was the target tug requirement that an additional 103 Lysander IIIA's were acquired from Britain (plus an odd II), most of which were converted to TT's in Canada. They bore RAF serials in the V block, but 57 (including our subject) were renumbered as RCAF 1536 to 1592. Most of the surviving II's joined the TT ranks when

the CAC Detachments were disbanded in late 1943. The Lysander TT's served in all eleven Bombing and Gunnery Schools and most of the OTU's. Their slow speed made them ideal for novice gunners but not as useful for operational training where target tugs with higher performance were desirable. They served until the BCATP was wound down and most were then sold as surplus. A number of the RCAF's 329 Lysanders have survived to be restored for display and demonstration purposes.

The Lysander Target Tug conversion focused largely on the rear cockpit where the guns and mounts were removed while the seat was moved aft to provide space for the winching gear and target drogue stowage. Externally the most visible change was removal of the ordnance-toting winglets on the main landing gear structure. Others included a rigid inverted tripod frame holding a pulley which allowed the target cable to be played out a safe distance below the empennage. The mechanical details of this feature and the internal winch gear were slightly different from those on tugs outfitted in the UK. As a further measure against cable and drogue fouling, a strut and wire arrangement was affixed to the underside of the horizontal tail just ahead of the tailwheel with similar wires to the vertical tail serving the same purpose above. A hatch immediately to the rear of the tripod frame allowed the operator to change drogues in flight. In its Canadian form, the TT conversion also featured a simple metal windshield ahead of the pulley and hatch plus a cabin-heat intensifier pipe installed within the exhaust pipe (interestingly, the short pipe leading from the intensifier rear junction to the cockpit is missing in the photos of 1579). The typical yellow and black of TT paint scheme has stripes at a 60 degree angle, with deviations here and there to allow for airframe features. Roundels are in all six positions are Type A. It should also be noted that the engine cowl on production Lysander III's and IIIA's featured identical fore and aft hasp assemblies to port, and two smaller lower bumps and a unique hinge arrangement to starboard. Some restored Lysanders appear to use the nearly similar Bolingbroke cowl, on which these features are noticeably different (see p.21 profiles).

Lysander IIIA V9521 was originally built for the RAF within the 10th production order for the type. Interestingly, some of the IIIAs from that 347 aircraft order also became the initial inventory of 414 RCAF Squadron overseas. V9521 was one of 57 Mk.IIIAs shipped to Canada for the express purpose of conversion to target tug configuration. It was TOS RCAF on 17 February 1942 and had been converted for its new role by 20 August. Presumably it carried its RCAF serial, 1579, from this date on. It was SOS on 12 June 1946. At a distance, the Mk.IIIA airframe was externally identifiable by its Lockheed tailwheel assembly. The Dowty unit on the original Mercury-engined Mk.IIIs featured a longer cuff around the upper part of the shock absorber oleo and a wider, smaller diameter tire. Other stock Mk.IIIA features were the new panel arrangement for the rear sliding canopy and lack of several hinged hatches on the rear fuselage to port. There were many other less visible equipment changes, some of which were in turn changed and modified ex-factory as required, determined by the type of unit the aircraft was destined for (i.e. Army Cooperation, Special Duties, Glider Tug or Target Tug).

Curtiss
Kittyhawk IV   Fighter

The Curtiss Kittyhawk shared the WWII air defence of Canada with the Hurricane [see p.18], each equipping the same number of squadrons. It may have received more publicity, however, because of some Kittyhawk units being deployed north to Alaska and often having more colourful markings than the RCAF's Hurricanes. This applied mostly to the early Kittyhawk I's, while the later Mk.III's and IV's have remained comparatively obscure.

The Kittyhawk (or USAAF P-40D to N) is well known as the first US fighter to be built in really large quantities and it served through most of the war with the USAAF and every other major Allied air arm. While it was widely regarded as having, at best, a mediocre performance; in most of the theatres in which it served it held its own or better and, in the hands of a really good pilot [see JF Edwards, p.64] it could rack up an exceptional score.

Strangely enough, the Kittyhawk was not the RCAF's first choice for an American fighter. This was the Bell P-39 Airacobra, a type whose estimated characteristics seemed to be just what the RCAF wanted, so much so that a licence for Canadian production was obtained in December 1940. To drastically condense the story, an order was placed by Canada with Bell for 144 Airacobras, but the British lusted for the type and ensured that the Canadian order kept getting shuffled to the bottom of the pile (at the end there were five British orders for 1075 Airacobras ahead of the Canadian!) while the license production plan had to be dropped because of engine shortages. After much argument, on 22 July 1941 Canada reluctantly agreed to accept 72 Kittyhawks diverted from RAF orders on the condition that they would be exchanged for 72 Airacobras as well as the remaining 72 on order, all by July 1942. Later, the RCAF negotiated a total exchange so the RAF could keep the Airacobras, even though by then the RAF had discovered it was not the wonder fighter that had been anticipated. In the event, the RCAF had received 72 Kittyhawk I's and 12 Mk.IA's between October 1941 and April 1942, at which point the arrangement with the British was abrogated by the Arnold-Towers-Portal agreement between the UK and US. Canada now had to apply for approval to purchase any US aircraft to the Joint Munitions Assignment Board, which eventually allotted 15 Mk.III's and 45 (later reduced to 35) Mk.IV's. Most of those came on RCAF strength between January 1943 and January 1944.

The first 84 Kittyhawks were issued to squadrons as fast as they were delivered. First, in November 41, was 118 (F) at Dartmouth, Nova Scotia, in Eastern Air Command which gratefully received them in exchange for their Grumman

text continued on p.58

Our subject aircraft is a veritable "black sheep" in the middle of this formation of Kittyhawk Mk.I stablemates. Not only is it the rarely seen Mk.IV (only 35 entered RCAF service), but it still carries its original USAAF paint scheme. The aircraft in the foreground is Kittyhawk Mk.I 1038 F. Other photos in the series show lots of cordite staining on the wings, indicating that this may have been the homeward bound end of a gunnery training sortie.

After 132 (F) disbanded in September of 1944, 877 was one of the Kittyhawks transferred to the Fighter Affiliation Flight of 5 OTU. Whether it was due to the desirability of being highly visible for this role or for maintenance reasons, the flight's fighters were stripped to natural metal. The serial was reapplied further back on the fuselage and two-letter codes beginning with the letter P were painted on the nose. The radiator intake lip was also painted with a dark colour, presumably black. The original camouflage colour remained on the upper nose to reduce glare. Other Kittyhawks of the flight had this area repainted matte black. Large portions of flaking and chipping suggest that overall paint removal work had a partial effect here as well. The stripping process also appears to have been abandoned on the vertical tail portion directly under the fin flash, a feature in common with other 5 OTU Kittyhawks.

This Kittyhawk IV was originally produced for the USAAF as P-40N-20-CU Warhawk serial number 43-23484 but was subsequently sold to Canada, entering RCAF inventory in late January 1944. Soon thereafter it was delivered to 132(F) Squadron. While it appears that minimal overpainting was done to obliterate its US serials and insignias, probably with the RCAF equivalents of RAF Dark Green on the upper surfaces and RAF Medium Sea Grey underneath, for the most part 877 retained its USAAF paint scheme of Olive Drab over Neutral Gray. The Medium Green wing and tail scallops, which often varied between aircraft batches, were also part of the scheme at this time. Standard Kittyhawk-sized RCAF roundels, fin flashes and serials were applied over this patchwork while unit-level markings comprised the aircraft-in-squadron code T (oddly obscuring part of the serial on both sides) and a maple leaf "zap" roundel to port. From late 1943 each WAC Kittyhawk squadron had a distinctive spinner colour, with 132 (F)'s being white.

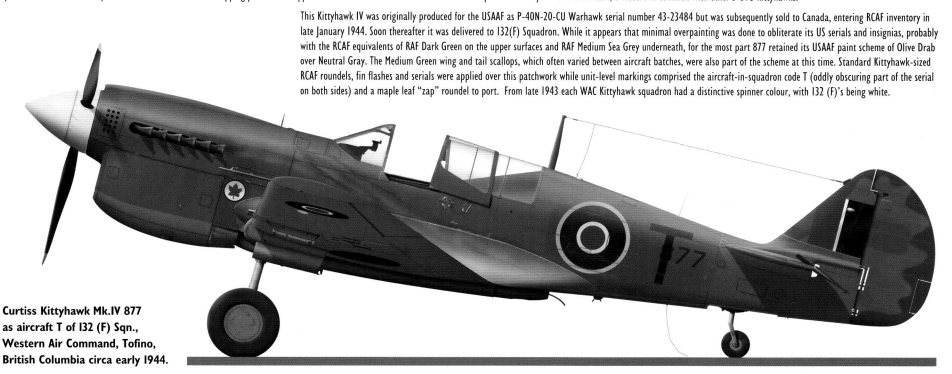

Curtiss Kittyhawk Mk.IV 877 as aircraft T of 132 (F) Sqn., Western Air Command, Tofino, British Columbia circa early 1944.

5 OTU Fighter Affiliation Flight Kittyhawks share the flight line with one of the unit's Mitchells. The 5 OTU Kittyhawks had several things in common with the unit's Liberators and Mitchells. All three were eventually stripped down to a bare metal finish. The two larger types had this done over a period of time, resulting in multi-finish flight lines, while the Kittyhawks all seem to have undergone the stripping process at once. Also, all 5 OTU aircraft were identified by a large two (or in the case of some Liberators single) letter code. The Kittyhawk codes all began with the letter P. Note the liberal flaking on the nose anti-glare area and the odd colouring on the vertical tail. It is possible that, as with some other 5 OTU Kittyhawks, the anti-glare area was later repainted matte black. Within a year of war's end, 877 was struck off charge, sold to a US civilian and registered N1009N.

Goblins. After this, three Kittyhawk squadrons were formed in succession at Rockcliffe - 111 (F) in November 1941 and 14 (F) and 132 (F) (the latter equipped with I A's) - in February and April 1942. All were transferred to Western Air Command as soon as possible – 111 (F) in December 1941 and 14 (F) and 132 (F) in March and June. The Japanese invasion of the Aleutians and the resulting threat to Alaska in June 1942 saw 111 (F) move north to mainland Alaska and thence to the Aleutians, where 14 (F) followed it in March 1943. Space prohibits a description of these two units' Aleutian exploits. Suffice it to say that, contrary to mythology, no RCAF Kittyhawk flew in action against the Japanese. Rather, the 111 (F) and 14 (F) pilots carried out these missions in USAAF or ex-USAAF P-40K's. In June 1942, as well, 118 (F) was rushed across the continent to Annette Island, Alaska. These three squadrons remained in Alaska until August/September 1943, when they returned to British Columbia and, in a few months, were sent overseas to fly Spitfires and Typhoons.

A former Army Cooperation squadron, 163 (F) also flew Kittyhawks in WAC from October 1943 to March 1944 when it was disbanded. Meanwhile, 132 (F), perhaps the quintessential WAC Kittyhawk squadron, spent most of its time at Tofino on the rainy and fog-shrouded west coast of Vancouver Island until disbanded on 30 September 1944. This meant that the fighter defence of British Columbia then devolved on 133 (F) and 135 (F), the last remaining WAC fighter squadrons, which had flown Hurricanes from late 1942 but in March 1944 re-equipped with Kittyhawks and moved to Patricia Bay. Here they saw out the war. Two 133 (F) Kittyhawks actually fired their guns in anger, shooting down a Japanese fire balloon each. There was one other RCAF Kittyhawk squadron for a brief period – 130 (F) – which was formed in May 1942 in EAC as the RCAF's first francophone squadron. It flew from Mont Joli during the Battle of the St. Lawrence, but by September it was converting to Hurricanes in Bagotville.

The Kittyhawk III's and IV's as they arrived were used to replace attrition in the mainland WAC squadrons and then largely equipped 133 (F) and 135 (F). When the latter became the last WAC fighter units, most of the remaining newer Kittyhawks were then used to form a Fighter Affiliation flight for 5 OTU. This unit, based at Boundary Bay and Abbotsford and equipped with Mitchells and Liberators was busy turning out crews for the RAF Liberator bomber squadrons in Southeast Asia. These were becoming increasingly Canadianized – at one point two thirds of 356 Squadron RAF's aircrew were RCAF! The Kittyhawks, flying from Boundary Bay, and stripped to bare metal, had a happy finale to their service, doing their best to keep the sprog Lib crewmen on their toes. Not simply simulating escorts, but enemy interceptors, the Kittyhawks made dummy attacks at all heights and from all angles. Indeed, one, 839, was destroyed in a mid-air collision with a Liberator. A number of the 5 OTU fighters, including 877, survived to become "warbirds" postwar.

Lockheed **Hudson I**
General Reconnaissance Aircraft

One of the more interesting aspects of the story of the 83 Lockheed Hudson I's and IIIA's employed by the RCAF's Home War Establishment [HWE] 1939-1945 was their acquisition. While coveted by the RCAF from the beginning and eventually becoming a mainstay of EAC, particularly in the Battles of the Atlantic and the St. Lawrence, they only came on strength as "substitutes" for the generally inferior Bristol Blenheim and Bolingbroke.

The broader story of the Hudson is well known. Ordered in 1938 by the RAF, following the cancellation of its Bolingbroke order (see p. 20), to supplement and eventually replace Coastal Command's Avro Ansons, it continued in production (2940 in all) for much of the war. It saw service in all theatres and in many roles and flew with the RAF, RAAF, RCAF, RNZAF and other allies, as well as the USAAF and a small (but highly successful) number with the USN. It was a straightforward military adaptation of the Lockheed 14 Super-Electra airliner.* It had many operational firsts including a U-boat forced to surrender by an RAF Hudson and the first sub kills by both the RCAF and USN. It was built in a number of variants, differing chiefly in equipment and power plant, though only to a minor extent.

In late August 1939, as war clouds loomed, the expanded Lockheed facility was still busy on the first Hudson contract – 200 for the RAF and 50 for the RAAF. A Canadian purchasing team, rushed down to the US in the last week of the month, was successful in ordering 20 Douglas B-18's (later known as Digbys in RCAF service) but, finding that Hudson production was booked up for months, made no further attempt to acquire the type. However, the RCAF was expecting bomber reinforcements. Nearly a year earlier, during the Munich crisis of September 1938, an earlier purchasing team had nearly signed a contract for 18 B-18's when the panic subsided. In the spring of 1939 the RCAF, which had naively forgotten the fact that it still had the money, suddenly came to, and, determined to spend it before Treasury Board caught on, placed an order in March 1939 for 18 Bristol Blenheim IV light bombers. At the start of the war these had been flight tested and were being crated for shipment to Canada to be issued to 7 (GP) Squadron with the proposed RCAF serials 720-737. With the declaration of war the UK, not knowing how the US Neutrality Act would affect Hudson deliveries, offered to allow Canada to purchase 18 of the Hudsons on order while the RAF would retain the Blenheims – an offer which was happily accepted at a total price of $2,340,000. [Note: the RCAF, which does not appear at its most alert in this whole affair, assumed that the Blenheim contract was cancelled but the UK considered it only postponed. Hence the Blenheims resurfaced a few months later, this time making it as far as the Halifax docks in June 1940. See p.22] The first ten Hudsons arrived in Canada before the country declared war on Germany on 10 September, although they did not formally come onto RCAF strength for a few more days. The US halted further shipments for a few weeks, until alterations in its neutrality legislation in November permitted a resumption. The remaining eight Hudsons plus another ten from the same batch which were purchased later reached Canada in early 1940. All were standard Mk.I's produced very close together and were allotted serials 759-786.

The first Hudsons were immediately issued to 11(BR) which had been formed from a nucleus of experienced RCAF personnel specifically to operate them. After a few weeks at Rockcliffe and Uplands in Ottawa the squadron moved to the new airfield at Dartmouth, Nova Scotia, its main base for most of the war. The unit's first operational flight from there was a naval cooperation exercise on 10 November. The remaining 18 Hudsons as they came on strength were used both to bring 11(BR) up to establishment, including a stored reserve, and to equip a flight of 13 (OT) Squadron at Patricia Bay, BC. At least one, 770, served with the RCAF HQ Communication Flight and crashed on 10 June 1940 at Newtonville, ON, killing Canadian Minister of National Defence Norman Rogers.

11(BR) had little difficulty in converting to the Hudson, successfully bringing them through the severe winter of 1939/40, while trying to reach an operational standard of efficiency in the new year. The Hudson I could carry an impressively varied bomb load – four 250 and three 100 pound (113 and 45 kg) anti-sub bombs plus eight 20 pound (9 kg) practice bombs is a load quoted by EAC. The unit did its best to follow the rather vague directions of RAF Coastal Command for a Hudson sub-attack – a shallow dive from 2000 feet (610 m), opening the bomb doors on sighting, as they took 16 seconds to open completely. In the

Hudson I N7349 picketed at Rockcliffe in early September 1939. The RCAF serial 764 has yet to be applied. Like our colour profile subject aircraft it was one of the early Hudson I's delivered without the Boulton Paul turret. Due to acquisition difficulties the initial RCAF (and RAAF as well) Hudsons would actually enter squadron service before the twin Browning .30cal equipped turrets could be acquired and installed. In the interim, some aircraft flew with flush metal skinning over the rear fuselage cutout while those of the initial delivery batch had a uniquely RCAF "greenhouse" cupola fitted. This view also shows the RAF position upper wing roundels and the overall excellent condition of the finish to good effect. The row of airliner-like windows down each side of the fuselage indicates the type's civilian heritage.

photo: LAC PL526

* Interestingly, the Hudson set a precedent for the adaptation of commercial airframes as excellent anti-sub aircraft several decades later, e.g. the Argus, Nimrod, Orion and Aurora – the latter two being a development of a later Lockheed Electra.

first few months 11(BR) dropped hundreds of practice bombs – singly, salvos, sticks – all at low level. Gun armament was lacking however. The Boulton Paul turrets had to be shipped from England and, since the RCAF had a very low priority, an RCAF-designed canopy occupied the dorsal position for many months.

The squadron and its Hudsons soldiered on at Dartmouth for two years with convoy escorts, patrols and training as its main activities. When 1(F) and its Hurricanes were rushed overseas to take part in the Battle of Britain 11(BR) also became responsible for the fighter defence of Halifax. In November 1941 part of the squadron moved even further into the front line with a four-plane detachment going to the nearly completed Torbay airfield near St. John's, Newfoundland. The new posting had its downside – the Canadians, ignoring local wisdom, had built their base in a location notorious for high winds and thick fog – and on occasion it could boast 50 knot winds and zero visibility simultaneously.

Early spring, 1940 at Dartmouth's barely completed new airfield. Hudson 762 moments after touchdown with the wing still carrying more weight than the wheels. The RCAFs interim cupola is clearly seen here, as are the type's massive flaps. Applied further inboard than the usual RCAF practice of the time, the underwing roundels are subtle evidence of the aircraft's RAF origin.

photo: LAC WRF160

Meanwhile the RCAF was desperately trying to build up its HWE, particularly EAC. Access to US production was by now resolutely blocked by the British, forcing it to rely on Canadian sources. Infuriatingly and simultaneously, the RCAF was about to take delivery of scores of brand new Hudsons, but these were as inaccessible to the EAC squadrons as if they had been owned by the *Luftwaffe*! They were destined for General Reconnaissance Schools and Operational Training Units [OTU] in the Maritimes and the barrier between the BCATP and the HWE was impenetrable. Fortunately, the RCAF was able to persuade the Air Ministry to release 55 Lend-Lease Hudson IIIA's to the HWE in exchange for Bolingbrokes for the BCATP [see p.23]. These new aircraft, which came on strength in early 1942, retained their RAF serials and were used to form 113 (BR) and to replace 119 (BR)'s Bolingbrokes and 8 (BR)'s Hudson I's.

In the meantime the Torbay detachment of 8 (BR) had exchanged the potent rum and attractive girls of St. John's for the better weather of Halifax and returned to Dartmouth and Hudson IIIA's. A new squadron, 145 (BR), formed at Torbay with EAC's surviving Hudson I's. The new Mk.IIIA's were a Godsend to EAC, but presented aircrew difficulties. The well-trained products

text continued on p.62

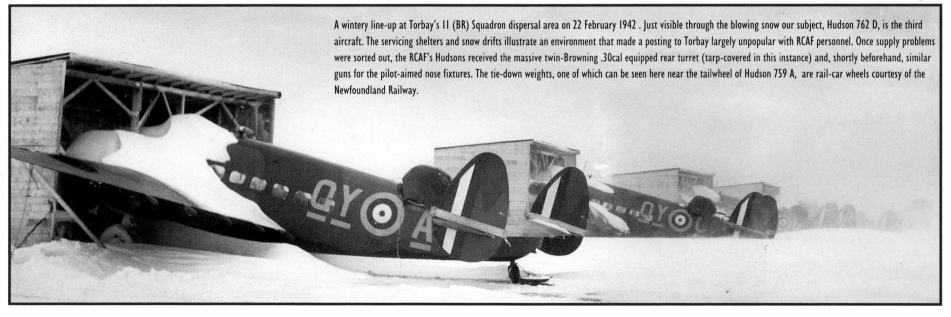

A wintery line-up at Torbay's 11 (BR) Squadron dispersal area on 22 February 1942 . Just visible through the blowing snow our subject, Hudson 762 D, is the third aircraft. The servicing shelters and snow drifts illustrate an environment that made a posting to Torbay largely unpopular with RCAF personnel. Once supply problems were sorted out, the RCAF's Hudsons received the massive twin-Browning .30cal equipped rear turret (tarp-covered in this instance) and, shortly beforehand, similar guns for the pilot-aimed nose fixtures. The tie-down weights, one of which can be seen here near the tailwheel of Hudson 759 A, are rail-car wheels courtesy of the Newfoundland Railway.

Carrying serial N7347, this aircraft was originally destined for the Royal Air Force under the Air Ministry's first Hudson direct purchase contract. Released to Canada (see main text), it became RCAF serial 762 a few days after delivery. Since the gun turrets for the US-made Hudsons were being manufactured in the UK, it made sense to have the aircraft delivered sans turret for installation after arrival. Thus, some of these first-contract RAF machines diverted to the RCAF were ferried north without even a makeshift cover for the turret station (see also p.59 photo). The illustration depicts the aircraft in ferry configuration with the relief crew cot folded up against the fuselage to port (as seen through the main cabin windows) and minimal radio equipment. Prior to entering squadron service, Commonwealth air force Hudsons had the cot removed to make way for IFF and other military equipment while new aerial wires appeared between the antenna mast, tail, and fuselage.

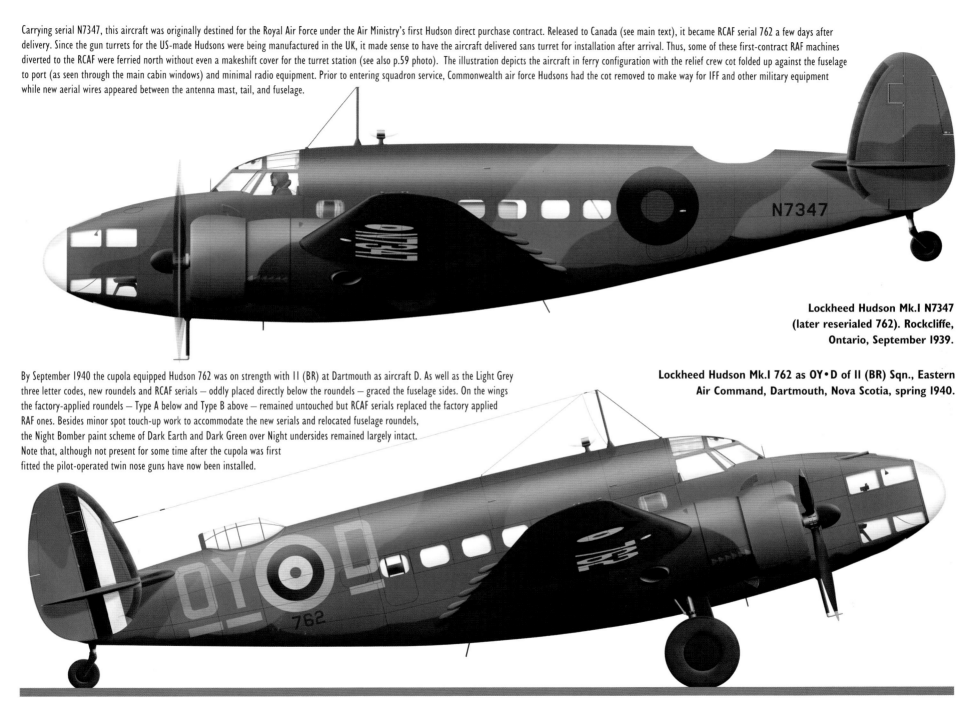

**Lockheed Hudson Mk.I N7347
(later reserialed 762). Rockcliffe,
Ontario, September 1939.**

By September 1940 the cupola equipped Hudson 762 was on strength with 11 (BR) at Dartmouth as aircraft D. As well as the Light Grey three letter codes, new roundels and RCAF serials — oddly placed directly below the roundels — graced the fuselage sides. On the wings the factory-applied roundels — Type A below and Type B above — remained untouched but RCAF serials replaced the factory applied RAF ones. Besides minor spot touch-up work to accommodate the new serials and relocated fuselage roundels, the Night Bomber paint scheme of Dark Earth and Dark Green over Night undersides remained largely intact. Note that, although not present for some time after the cupola was first fitted the pilot-operated twin nose guns have now been installed.

**Lockheed Hudson Mk.I 762 as OY•D of 11 (BR) Sqn., Eastern
Air Command, Dartmouth, Nova Scotia, spring 1940.**

Left: 762 in its new ASW paint scheme as 145(BR) aircraft EA•D operating from Torbay, 1 October 1942. Devised initially to delay enemy visual acquisition of an incoming patrol aircraft, this finish had the secondary benefit of temporarily confusing the enemy's naval AA crews (the smaller silhouette against a typical North Atlantic sky making the distance appear greater than it really was) during those crucial first moments of an engagement. Interestingly, the special white coating devised to tone down the contrast of the rubber deicer boots (see also Sunderland p.14) has also been extended to the tires in this case. This Hudson I was still with145 (BR) when it crashed on 9 July 1943.

photo: LAC PL117987

Below: Loading the roomy bomb bay of a 113(BR) Hudson Mk.IIIA with early-production Mk.XI depth charges at Yarmouth. A typical ASW patrol load was 4x 250lb d/cs along with various marker pyrotechnics. Though smaller than the 450lb naval depth charge first adapted for aerial use by the RAF, RN-FAA, and RCAF, the purpose-designed 250lb aerial d/c was a much more effective weapon. In both the initial Mk.VIII and the evolved Mk.XI form, it accounted for more U-boats being put out of action — temporarily or permanently — than any other aircraft-launched weapon of the war.

of the Operational Training Units were also not for EAC but for Coastal Command. So it was that EAC had to crew the much-increased Hudson force with men just out of Service Flying Training School [SFTS], a task not eased by the fact that there were just three sets of Hudson dual controls in the entire command. Pointing out the U-boat actions now being confronted and begging to borrow some from the BCATP units, EAC's "Required most urgently, repeat, most urgently" elicited little response until a couple were borrowed from the USAAF at McCord Field. Space prohibits following the RCAF Mk.III's in detail – suffice it to say that they served EAC well until mid 1944, saw much action and one was responsible for EAC's first kill, U-754 [see p.20].

Meanwhile, 145(BR) took over the Hudson I's, which were in their third year of arduous service, and operated them for another year. That period was a non-stop struggle to keep the old Mk.I's serviceable. Even the Navy expressed concern at their condition! Nonetheless, they kept going and did their duty – Hudson 760 attacked U-69 which had earlier sunk the Newfoundland-Canada ferry *Caribou* on 21 October, but without success. On 30 and 31 October, however, in the battle for convoy SC-107, the squadron made two attacks, both by Hudson 784, in the first sinking U-658, in the second damaging U-521. Although gradually supplemented by a few Mk.III's, the Mk.I's continued to take most of the load, but at a price – 760 crashed and exploded ahead of a convoy on 28 January and 771 took off on 14 February and disappeared forever. The first Venturas arrived in May 1943 and the

Hudsons were gradually phased out. One of the last to go was our subject aircraft, Hudson I 762, which, returning from a ferry flight on 9 July, crashed at Charlottetown in the course of a single-engined forced landing. The engine failure may have been caused by ground crew unfamiliarity with a Mk.I Hudson. 762, the RCAF's fourth Hudson, had served the RCAF faithfully for nearly four years.

By the time it was part of the detachment at Torbay in early 1942, Hudson 762 had finally received its turret. These were installed progressively while the squadron was fully operational — photos exist showing turretless and turreted aircraft together both in formation and on the hardstand. Right from the factory, the Boulton Paul C.II turrets were painted Night overall. Most operators did not alter this on installation, but later in their service life both RAF Coastal Command and RCAF HWE Hudsons that were repainted with later ASW schemes often had the finish on their turrets overpainted in White.

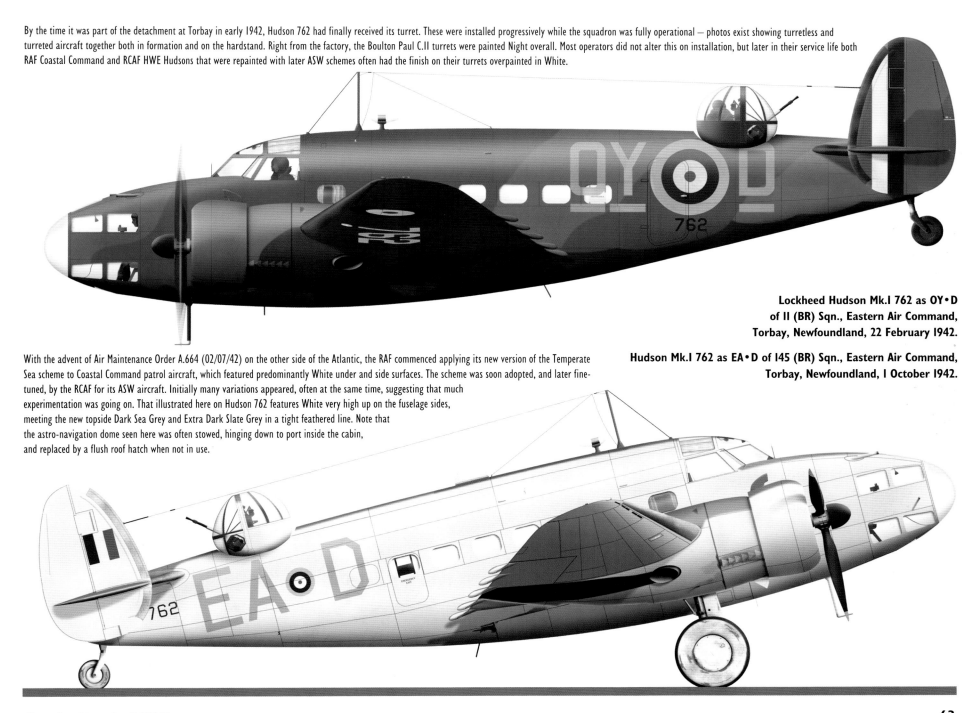

Lockheed Hudson Mk.I 762 as OY•D of II (BR) Sqn., Eastern Air Command, Torbay, Newfoundland, 22 February 1942.

With the advent of Air Maintenance Order A.664 (02/07/42) on the other side of the Atlantic, the RAF commenced applying its new version of the Temperate Sea scheme to Coastal Command patrol aircraft, which featured predominantly White under and side surfaces. The scheme was soon adopted, and later fine-tuned, by the RCAF for its ASW aircraft. Initially many variations appeared, often at the same time, suggesting that much experimentation was going on. That illustrated here on Hudson 762 features White very high up on the fuselage sides, meeting the new topside Dark Sea Grey and Extra Dark Slate Grey in a tight feathered line. Note that the astro-navigation dome seen here was often stowed, hinging down to port inside the cabin, and replaced by a flush roof hatch when not in use.

Hudson Mk.I 762 as EA•D of 145 (BR) Sqn., Eastern Air Command, Torbay, Newfoundland, 1 October 1942.

Wing Commander "Stocky" Edwards
Spitfire & Fw190
Fighter & "war prize"

From time immemorial, leaders in battle have made their personal mounts distinctive, both for easy identification in battle and, frequently, to express their own flamboyant personalities. This custom persisted into the air age, with results that have ranged from the discreetly functional to the bizarre. In the case of the Royal Air Force and associated formations during the Second World War, the most prominent and consistent example was for the leaders of fighter wings to identify their aircraft with their own initials, rather than the code letters of one of the wing's squadrons. Possibly the practice was started by the near-legendary Douglas Bader who carried the initials D·B on his Spitfire as leader of the Tangmere Wing in early 1941. Whether this is so, at what point the custom became common practice and when (if at all) and in what form it became officially sanctioned is, at present, unknown to the author. Suffice it to say that by the end of the war a fair number of Canadians both in the RCAF and RAF had commanded fighter wings and sported their initials on their aircraft.

Another aircraft category which some wing leaders monogrammed were captured enemy machines. Normally these were adopted by the unit but occasionally the wing leader would glaum onto one – usually a liaison type (Bf108 *Taifun's* were popular) – but sometimes an operational type, if for no other reason than to try the paces of a former opponent.

In this AviaDossier we have chosen, as an example of this practice, an outstanding Canadian fighter pilot and leader, the desert ace JF Edwards, variously nicknamed "Eddie" or "Stocky."

Born and raised in Saskatchewan, Edwards joined the RCAF in October 1940 at the age of 19. His progress followed the normal path of elementary and service flying training in Canada, and, after being selected as a prospective fighter pilot, OTU training on Hurricanes in the UK. Having qualified he was posted to North Africa and, like many RCAF airmen during the war, joined an RAF unit, 94 Squadron, as a sergeant pilot. Here on 2 March 1942 he scored his first victory in the aircraft with which he is most associated – the Curtiss Kittyhawk. The Kittyhawk [see p.56] was a sturdy aircraft with a reasonable performance at

James "Stocky" Edwards strikes a pose for an official RCAF photographer circa early May 1945. His Spitfire, although a relatively new one, has all the hallmarks of an operational machine; grime from vital fluids and exhaust plus some chipping and scrubbing of entry area paint. The odd darker, refinishing on the lower nose, extending loosely below the cowl panel line, and onto the port wing seems to have been a feature common to the paintwork of a number of later Castle Bromwich-produced Mk.XVIs. With the war nearly over, the young wing commander still chalked up 54 operational sorties during his relatively short time (6 April to 7 July 1945) with 127 Wing.

photo: W/C J.F. "Stocky" Edwards

low and medium level. However, both engine and armament were affected by desert conditions and it was never considered a real match for most Axis fighters. Despite this, Edwards' superb gunnery skills, particularly in deflection shooting, and exceptional flying ability more than balanced the scales.

Space prohibits all but the briefest resumé of his combat career which has been recounted elsewhere. To summarize, after a brief period with 94 he joined 260 Squadron and flew fighter and ground attack sorties for 13 months as the battlefront seesawed back and forth across Libya and into Tunisia. By the end of the North African war he had at least 13 ½ aerial victories, all fighters, as well as a number of probables plus many aircraft and vehicles destroyed on the ground.* He is credited with a victory over Otto Schulz,

one of the *Luftwaffe's* leading *experten* in Africa on 17 June 1942. He did a second tour on Spitfires in Italy, where he rose to command a squadron and added 3 FW190's to his total. After his second tour and a brief stay in Canada he was promoted to Wing Commander and on 6 April 1945 became Wing Leader of 127 Wing, RCAF. The war was nearly over, but he was still able to claim an Me262 and an FW190 damaged plus a share in a Ju88.

In 1971 he retired after a distinguished postwar RCAF career. At the time of writing (July 2009) W/C JF Edwards, DFC & Bar, DFM is the highest-scoring RCAF fighter ace still living. Long may he remain so.

---

* A relatively small proportion of this total – ⅓ of a full claim – was for the shared destruction of an Me323 transport.

Supermarine Spitfire Mk.XVI TD147 as JF•E of 127 (Fighter) Wing RCAF (commander's aircraft), 2nd Tactical Air Force base B.154 (Schneverdingen - Soltau) Spring / Summer, 1945.

Spitfire LF.XVIE TD147 was a late production version of the Packard Merlin 266 powered Mark XVI, completed by Vickers-Armstrong at Castle Bromwich in early 1945. From there it went to 9 MU in early March, prior to being issued to 443 Squadron RCAF at Eindhoven, Netherlands, on 5 April 1945. The very next day James Edwards became the Wing Commander (Flying) of 443's parent unit, 127 (Fighter) Wing. This Spitfire soon became his personal mount, though the Wing Commander did inherit the Mk.IX of Johnnie Johnson (his predecessor in 127 Wing) complete with ground crew, and flew it on occasion. The new commander often led missions ranging from tactical support and transport escort to armed recce (free hunts for any viable military targets). On one mission, while attacking enemy shipping at Kiel, AA fire knocked the left-hand cannon and its attendant structure out of the Spitfire he was flying. So serious was the damage to the wing, that the aircraft was declared u/s soon after landing. Edwards damaged both an Fw190 and an Me262 in a single sortie while flying TD147 on 29 April 1945. The illustration depicts this aircraft bombed up for a typical fighter-bomber sortie with a 250lb MC bomb under each wing and a 45 gallon drop tank under the belly. In lieu of the belly tank, a 500lb bomb could be carried. After June of 1945 TD147 appears to have entered long term storage, showing up in the inventory of the Royal Hellenic Air Force by the summer of 1949. Externally, the Packard Merlin 266 powered Spitfire Mk.XVI was virtually indistinguishable from the Rolls Royce Merlin 66 powered Mk.IX. All Mk.XVIs appear to have featured the larger rudder and the E wing armament (2x 20mm cannon and 2x .50 calibre machine guns), whereas the Mk.IX could have combinations of either rudder type plus either the C or E wing [see pp.46-47]. The camouflage scheme is also similar in pattern and identical in paint specification to other late war Spitfires serving in Northwest Europe.

Another view of JF•E taken, presumably, on the same day as the photo at left. This photo reveals yet more of the general condition of the finish, including the usual exhaust and oil staining and — barely visible — a certain amount of combat flying induced stress accenting the rear fuselage rivet lines.

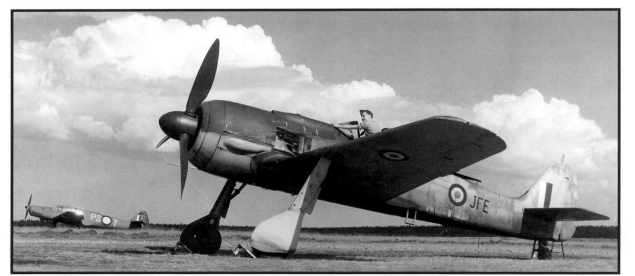

JFE marks this Fw190 as James F. Edwards' war prize while his fellow-Canadian friend, and boss at the time, Group Captain Percival "Stan" Turner has his PST brand on the more sedate Bf108 *Taifun* in the background. The photo, reported to have been taken not too long after VE Day, reveals features of most of the new management's paintwork. The lighter colour sprayed over the *Luftwaffe* markings on the lower wings, fuselage and tail is most probably Sky, as the standard RAF stock colour for undersides at the time — Medium Sea Grey — should have appeared a little darker than the standard Luftwaffe fighter base colour, RLM76 Light Blue. It is conceivable that ample stocks of Sky would have been on hand since Spitfire squadron code letters were all painted in that colour.

Focke Wulf Fw190F-8 Wk.Nr 933849,
127 Wing RCAF, Soltau, Germany, May/June 1945.

Stocky Edwards remembers first seeing this Fw190 sitting abandoned in a field while he was returning to base one day. On landing he sent flight commander "Cap" Foster, accompanied by ground crew, to drive out to the nearby field and investigate, with orders to fly it back to base if possible. Before long it had the Wing Commander's initials and RAF official insignia applied over the crosses and *swastikas*. Edwards himself logged 4 hops in it, and even several against it, with 443 Squadron commander Hart Finley flying opposite, testing the erstwhile enemy against their Spitfires. Lasting impressions include "a well designed cockpit" and "superb ground handling." Within two weeks Group HQ brass had caught wind of the aircraft's presence and whisked it away. Other than it being a Dornier-built machine, little could be discovered about Wk.Nr. 933849's *Luftwaffe* history. W/C Edwards recalls that it may have had some connection with a nearby *Luftwaffe* test unit. The apparent lack of unit markings — the areas fore and aft of the fuselage cross were not overpainted - and relatively fresh nature of the finish on the prop and cowl would indicate that it was not an extensively used aircraft. In 127 Wing hands it received some lighter paint atop the *Luftwaffe* markings, otherwise leaving the original German RLM74/75/76 finish and much of the factory-applied *Werke Nummer* intact. Although this photo was most certainly taken in late May or early June of 1945, the roundels and fin flash resemble the later postwar RAF style, albeit in wartime colours. Note that the usual 190F *Jabo* bomb racks, wing cannon, nose guns, and wire radio aerial are not present, though the cannon and guns were still aboard when this aircraft was flown in.

Sources and Select Bibliography

The research upon which this book is based is, as with most historical writing, a progression from the general to the particular. This normally takes the form of a movement from published to primary sources.

For *Canadian Aircraft of WWII*, published sources focus on an absolutely essential trinity:

J.A Griffin, *Canadian Military Aircraft Serials & Photographs 1920-1968*, Queen's Printer, Ottawa, Ontario, 1969

Kostenuk, S., and J. Griffin, *RCAF Squadrons and Aircraft*, Hakkert, Toronto, 1977

Molson, K.W., and H.A. Taylor, *Canadian Aircraft since 1904*, Canada's Wings, Stittsville, Ontario, 1982

These give a complete and reasonably accurate coverage of RCAF aircraft inventory, RCAF organization and Canadian aircraft production for the period.

In the case of the organization, administration, policy, procurement and, particularly, operations, the current researcher is fortunate in the appearance over the last two decades of several volumes of the RCAF Official History and, in the case of the maritime air war, the equivalent for the RCN:

Douglas, W.A.B, *The Creation of a National Air Force: The Official History of the Royal Canadian Air Force, Volume II*, University of Toronto Press, Toronto, Ontario, 1986

Greenhous, Brereton, Stephen J. Harris, William C. Johnston and William G.P. Rawling, *The Crucible of War, 1939-1945: The Official History of the Royal Canadian Air Force, Volume III*, University of Toronto Press, Toronto, Ontario, 1994

Douglas, W.A.B., Roger Sarty and Michael Whitby, *No Higher Purpose: The Official Operational History of the Royal Canadian Navy in the Second World War, 1939-1940, Volume II, Part 1*, Vanwell, St. Catharines, Ontario, 2002

..... *A Blue Water Navy: The Official Operational History of the Royal Canadian Navy in the Second World War, 1939-1940, Volume II, Part 2*, Vanwell, St. Catharines, Ontario, 2007

These are massive tomes, well researched and written, essential to but often ignored by aviation writers.

For the actual design and progressive development of the aircraft themselves the author has had recourse to literally hundreds of books, most published in the US and UK and devoted either exclusively or in part to the type concerned. For the most part their accuracy is high though any Canadian coverage is liable to be incomplete or unreliable.

The main documentary sources for the work are the records held by Library and Archives Canada and its predecessors and, to a lesser degree, those still in the possession of the Department of National Defence. These include the records of the RCAF, both operational and technical as well as general, of the Department of Munitions and Supply and of Parliament. Specific coverage of operational events relies heavily on the diaries and operational records of the squadrons and other formations concerned. All information initially derived from published sources was employed as part of the narrative structure only until it could, where possible, be confirmed, amended or, all too frequently, eliminated or replaced, after being compared to the official documentation. It is safe to say that the great majority of the statements in the textual narrative have undergone this process.

Glossary

2nd Tactical Air Force: This high level formation was first formed 1 June 1943 with the goal of providing a coordinated multi-role force to provide air superiority over, and air support of, land formations on the move during the Allied invasion of Europe in the following year. Originating with Army Cooperation Command, it added units drawn from both Fighter and Bomber Commands. It evolved into the British Air Forces of Occupation (BAFO) soon after the end of fighting in Europe.

acoustic torpedo: Self-powered, sound-guided weapons launched by aircraft, ships and submarines. While the German Navy pioneered their use in submarines against surface vessels, only the Allies had an aircraft-launched type throughout WWII (see p.36 sidebar).

(British) Air Ministry: Department of the British Government responsible for the affairs of the Royal Air Force. In existence from 1918 to1964.

(Avro) Anson: An RAF twin-engined aircraft originally (1935) developed for the maritime general reconnaissance role, but later produced in great numbers in the UK and Canada for training and communications.

Army Cooperation Command: RAF Command (December 1940-May 1943) responsible for operational activities involving interaction between the Army and the RAF.

Arnold-Towers-Portal agreement: One of a series of US-UK agreements (1942) concerning the allocation of aircraft production and the role of the Joint Munitions Assignment Board.

A/S bomb: Antisubmarine bomb. Developed throughout the 1930s for the RAF Coastal Command's then emerging ASW mission. The evolved Mk.III and IV designs, featuring anti-ricochet "flower pot" nose caps and available in 100, 250, and 500 lb sizes, entered the inventory in late 1938. An earlier, smaller 35lb version was also still then in service. Detonation was accomplished by impact sensitive short-delay (usually 1 sec.) pistols or, later, by hydrostatic fuzes preset for 18, 23, or 30 foot depths. A/S bombs were the RAF's only dedicated ASW ordnance in use at the start of WWII. Distinct from these is the late-war 600lb A/S bomb which was more like a depth charge (see).

ASG: RCAF designation for American 10-centimetre wavelength radar.

ASV: An official British designator, and often the common descriptor, for Air to Surface Vessel radar , which saw progressive improvements from Mk.I through to Mk.IV during WWII.

ASW: Antisubmarine warfare.

(Fairey) Battle: A single-engined RAF light bomber of the early war years which later saw service as a trainer and target tug, particularly in Canada.

Battle of the Atlantic: General description of the campaign to keep the sea-lanes open between the UK and North and South America.

Battle of the St. Lawrence: Description of the incursions of U-boats into the Gulf of St. Lawrence and the St. Lawrence River from May through October 1942 and the RCAF and RCN's efforts to combat them.

beaching gear: wheeled devices purpose-built for specific flying boat types, used to handle and marshal these aircraft on land.

(Bristol) Beaufort: A British twin-engined strike and torpedo bomber aircraft evolved in part from the Blenheim/Bolingbroke and used as the basis for the later Beaufighter.

Black Pit: That part of the North Atlantic beyond the operational range of aircraft based in the UK, Iceland and Newfoundland.

(Bristol) Blenheim: A British twin-engined light bomber that entered service in its Mk.I form in 1937. The later, longer-nosed Mk.IV was very similar to the earlier general reconnaissance Bolingbroke. Equipped with a gun pack beneath the bomb bay, each Mark became a fighter as the Mk.IF and the Mk.IVF. The later Mk.V was a development of the Mk.IV.

Boeing Aircraft of Canada Ltd.: Aircraft manufacturing company based in Vancouver, BC.

Bomber Command: RAF command responsible for UK-based bomber operations.

Bowden cable: A coaxial cable used to transmit mechanical energy to a remote device. A familiar example is the bicycle brake cable.

British Purchasing Mission: Body responsible in the first years of the war for purchasing military materials in the US.

Browning M2: A long-lived US machine gun design. The .30 calibre version as used in aircraft was re-engineered from the M1919 infantry

machine gun, optimized for high speed air cooling and higher rates of fire, emerged as the M2. Two versions – the Mk.I and Mk.II – were rechambered for British .303.
The .50 calibre Browning has always carried the M2 designator since service entry (1933). Models of both calibers were manufactured by Birmingham Small Arms (BSA) for British Service use.

Cabot Strait: Body of water between Southwest Newfoundland and Nova Scotia.

Canadian Vickers: Montreal-based ship-building and aircraft manufacturing company.

Canpay: Arrangement by which Canada paid for military purchases in the US.

Chance Vought: American aircraft manufacturing company.

Coastal Command: RAF command responsible for all aspects of maritime warfare.

Confederation: Union of Newfoundland with Canada, 1 April 1949.

de Havilland: British aircraft manufacturing company.

de Havilland Canada: Toronto-based Canadian aircraft manufacturing company.

Department of Munitions and Supply: Canadian government department responsible for controlling the production and purchase of war material during WWII.

depth charge (a.k.a. d/c): A thin-walled explosive device featuring a high charge to overall weight ratio and hydrostatic triggering first developed by the Royal Navy for ASW in WWI. The basic ship-launched 450 lb Mk.VII device in service at the beginning of WWII was adapted for aerial use by affixing carriage lugs and later, aerodynamic nose and tail fairings. Still later, specially designed aerial depth charges in the 250 lb class offered more tactical flexibility in featuring higher yield explosives (ultimately Torpex) and better shallow-depth triggering. Proving more effective overall, they had almost entirely replaced the A/S bomb in frontline use by late 1942.
Curiously, the late-war 600 lb A/S bomb (see) was, if the charge/weight ratio and triggering mechanism type are defining parameters, a depth charge designed to tolerate higher speed and higher altitude drops, intended to counter, from a safer altitude, U-boats fighting back.
In US parlance a "depth charge" is used exclusively by naval vessels while that dropped by aircraft is a "depth bomb."

DF loop: A loop-shaped antenna used by an aircraft's radio direction finding system.

(Douglas) Digby: The RCAF name for a twin-engined medium-heavy bomber produced pre-war for the USAAC. Twenty were purchased by Canada and used by 10 (BR) 1939-1943 in the Maritime patrol ASW role.

DTD: The British Air Ministry's Directorate of Technical Development. The organisation responsible for the specification and establishment of technical standards ranging from airframe construction materials and instruments to finish coatings and consumables like fuels and lubricants. Its origins can be traced back to the former Directorate of Research, which had split into several more specialized directorates, including this one, in the mid 1920s. The post of Director was traditionally held by an appointed high-ranking RAF officer.

experten: Expert. Luftwaffe equivalent to ace.

Fairchild Aircraft Ltd.: Canadian aircraft manufacturing company located at Longueil, Quebec.

Fighter Command: RAF command responsible for fighter operations.

Fleet Aircraft Ltd: A Canadian aircraft manufacturing company based at Fort Erie, Ontario.

Grumman Goblin: RCAF name for a version of the 1931 Grumman FF-1 two seat biplane carrier-based fighter. Assembled at Canadian Car and Foundry for the Spanish Republic in 1938, 16 undelivered examples were acquired with extreme reluctance by the RCAF in 1940.

Handley Page Hampden: RAF twin-engined medium bomber and torpedo bomber, also used in RCAF squadrons in both the HWE and overseas.

Joint Munitions Assignment Board: A joint UK/US body responsible for determining the allocation of war production to the Allied nations.

Lend-Lease: An abbreviation for US legislation by which US war material was purchased for the US armed forces but supplied to various Allied nations. Canada was not one of these. It was, however, a supplier of Lend-Lease materiel.

Lewis gun: Generally refers to a range of light machine guns originating with a pre WWI American design. In the context of WWII aircraft, it usually refers to the Lewis Aircraft Pattern Mk.III, IV, or V as manufactured by

Birmingham Small Arms (BSA) and chambered for the British .303 cartridge.

Lord Beaverbrook: William Maxwell "Max" Aitken, a Canadian of Scottish heritage who pursued a journalistic career in the UK with great success becoming a "press baron." Also active in politics, he became a peer in 1917. He was Minister of Information in 1918, while during WWII he became the first Minister of Aircraft Production and later Minister of Supply.

Ministry of Aircraft Production (MAP): One of several specialized supply ministries set up by the British government in WWII, and responsible for the production of aircraft through most of the war.
Note: Paint schemes and paint colours named with capitalised terms (eg. "Temperate Sea Scheme" or "Sky") throughout this book indicate that they are official MAP specification titles.

Munich crisis: A period during September 1938 when a European war was feared because of the threatened German aggression against Czechoslovakia. An agreement signed in Munich gained temporary peace but left the Czechs defenceless.

Narvik **class:** A class of very large German destroyers, unofficially called "the Narvik flotilla" as it was thought they were to replace the destroyers lost at Narvik in 1940.

National Research Council (NRC): Founded in 1916, the National Research Council was and is the Canadian government's principal science and technology research agency.

(US) Neutrality Act: This 1939 United States legislation was the last in a series of Acts designed to limit and control the export of US war material to foreign belligerents.

OTU: Operational Training Unit. A type of organization within all Commonwealth air arms, including the RCAF's HWE and BCATP, designed to train each aircrew member in the duties involved in actual operations against the enemy. Some OTUs have gone over to actual combat operations from time to time.

Paukenschlag: Codeword, meaning Drumbeat, for the U-boat offensive against North America after US entry into WWII.

RCAF Station Gander: The RCAF station at the Newfoundland Airport, Gander, Newfoundland.

(Hawker) Sea Hurricane: Versions of the Hurricane fighter designed for shipboard use by the Royal Navy's Fleet Air Arm.

SFTS: Service Flying Training School. A BCATP school designed to instruct pilots in airmanship beyond the elementary level.

SOS: Struck off Strength. When an aircraft is officially removed from the responsibility of a unit, e.g. Squadron, School. This normally involves a transfer, but when it is SOS RCAF, it is permanently written off (see also TOS).

Test and Development Establishment: Formerly Test and Development Flight. RCAF organization responsible for testing new or modified aircraft and equipment.

Torpex: TORpedo EXplosive. A secondary explosive (i.e. a primer or detonator is needed to activate) developed by Britian's Royal Gunpowder Factory specifically to maximize the underwater shock effect of its explosive pulse. Its energy output was reportedly 1.5 times that of a TNT charge of the same weight. It entered production in late 1942 and was in widespread use in depth charges, mines, torpedoes and deep-penetration bombs by mid 1943.

TOS: Taken on Strength (see also SOS).

Treasury Board: An arm of the Canadian Cabinet primarily responsible for the allocation of government funds and monitoring their expenditure.

Ubat: U-boat attack.

U-boat: From the German *Unterseeboot.* A submarine in the German Navy.

(Lockheed) Ventura: A combat aircraft based on the L-18 Lodestar. Larger and more powerful than its predecessor, the Hudson, it fulfilled similar roles from about mid 1942 onwards in the RAF, USAAF, USN and other allied air arms including the RCAF HWE.

VGO Gun: Alternately, Vickers K Gun – Vickers Gas Operated. A drum-fed light machine gun which used the .303 British cartridge. It was employed as aircraft defensive armament and, in limited numbers, for use on land vehicles. It was introduced on British military aircraft as a faster-firing successor to the Lewis Gun. The VGO was eventually outmoded by the Browning M2.

Wk.Nr. (Werke Nummer): Works Number… the factory serial number on German aircraft.

Appendix 1: RCAF Higher Formations

As mentioned in the Introduction, during the Second World War the Royal Canadian Air Force operated in several spheres of activity which made its organisation, if not unique, at least quite distinctive. The following concise summaries – though not entirely comprehensive – cover the main features, particularly of those for the formations that actually operated aircraft.

The Home War Establishment

This was responsible for units and operations in North America and was that part of the RCAF over which Headquarters had the greatest control. The largest operational units were the two Commands - Eastern and Western Air Commands, which were responsible for operations on the Atlantic and Pacific coasts respectively. While in RAF practice both Commands and the immediately subordinate formations (Groups) were functional (e.g. Bomber, Fighter), in the RCAF they designated area-oriented organisations. While each of the main RCAF commands controlled their respective areas, they also acted as operational group headquarters for most of their subordinate units. However, several actual groups did exist in the HWE. The longest standing and most important was 1 Group in EAC with HQ at St. John's, Newfoundland. It functioned from July 1941 to the end of the war and was responsible for operations over the Northwest Atlantic, Newfoundland and Labrador. Also in EAC was 5 (Gulf) Group which existed from late spring to autumn in both 1943 and 1944 to control antisubmarine operations over the Gulf of St Lawrence during the shipping season. In WAC, 4 Group was responsible for units in northern BC and the Yukon from June 1942 to April 1944. There were only two wings in the HWE, which also were regional rather than functional - X Wing which comprised the two RCAF squadrons based in northern Alaska and the Aleutians and Y Wing which consisted of the two squadrons on Annette Island in southern Alaska.

The basic aircraft-operating unit was the squadron. The RCAF started the war with eight in the HWE and at its peak, in late 1943, had 55. This number diminished between January 1944 and August 1945 as squadrons were disbanded or transferred overseas. The smallest independent unit was the detachment - either a temporary portion of a squadron operating separately, or, in the case of the six Coast Artillery Cooperation Detachments as an independent unit. Most squadrons or detachments were controlled directly by Commands or the few groups and wings. Several, however, were under the direct command of RCAF Headquarters.

British Commonwealth Air Training Plan

A large proportion of the RCAF's North American effort during the Second World War was the implementation of the agreement signed on 17 December 1939 which resulted in the British Commonwealth Air Training Plan (BCATP). The magnitude of Canada's role is illustrated by the fact that 45% of all Commonwealth airmen trained during the war undertook all or part of their training in Canada. Also, all aircraft became the property of the administrator – Canada – so that more than 90% of the aircraft that came on the strength of the RCAF during WWII were used by the BCATP.

The BCATP in Canada was separated, from east to west into four commands, 3, 1, 2, and 4 Training Commands. The basic unit within these commands was the school. The largest percentage of these were Elementary Flying Training Schools and Service Flying Training Schools – 29 of each – as well as 10 Air Observer Schools, 11 Bombing and Gunnery Schools, four Wireless Schools, two Air Navigation Schools, two General Reconnaissance Schools, two Flying Instructor Schools, a Naval Air Gunnery School, a Central Flying School and a Central Navigation School. Some were operated by the RCAF, others were operated by civilian contractors, and there were also RAF schools which had been moved to Canada. All were administered by the RCAF. In addition were seven large Operational Training Units which prepared aircrew for various categories of operational flying. When, due to its great success, the BCATP began to downsize in late 1944, most of the operational training units continued until the end of the war.

The RCAF Overseas

During the Second World War, RCAF Overseas Headquarters exercised administrative control over all RCAF personnel and units overseas. Two thirds of the former served with the RAF, and hence are beyond the scope of this book. Of these units, as with the HWE, the basic formation was the squadron. These consisted of three regular and reserve squadrons sent to the UK in 1940, 35 Article 15* squadrons formed in the UK from personnel trained under the BCATP, six HWE fighter squadrons transferred to the UK in late 1943 and three air observation post units created in the last month of the war – 47 altogether. The nine squadrons sent from Canada initially bore their original RCAF numbers, but in order to avoid confusion with RAF units all RCAF squadrons were eventually given consecutive numbers beginning with 400. The squadrons were of all types, and while the majority served in the UK or subsequently in Northwest Europe, a number served in the Mediterranean theatre or in the Far East.

While Overseas Headquarters strove mightily to create a more rational overseas RCAF structure by creating distinct RCAF superior formations such as wings and groups, it achieved this with only a moderate degree of success; certainly less than the Canadian Army. There were for a time, however, two Canadian fighter wings in Fighter Command and, subsequently, three fighter wings, two fighter bomber wings and one reconnaissance wing in the Second Tactical Air Force as well as a temporary medium bomber wing in North Africa. The largest RCAF formation overseas was 6 (RCAF) Group of RAF Bomber Command which at its peak operated 13 heavy bomber squadrons as well as three Heavy Conversion Units.

Article 15 of the BCATP Agreement may be viewed as the cutting edge of the RCAF's attempt to maintain as much autonomy as possible. It was hotly disputed at the time the agreement was drafted and the result – a compromise – allowed the Dominion air forces to form overseas squadrons from graduates of the plan. The RCAF's allotment was 25, later increased to 35, the RAAF's 17 and the RNZAF's 5.*

Appendix 2: U-boat encounters referred to in this volume

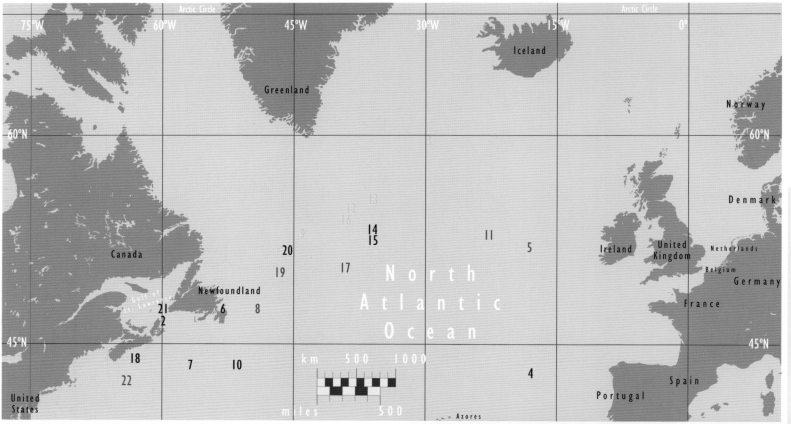

Map showing the position of encounters with U-boats referred to in this volume, listed in order of page-number occurrence. Yellow numbers indicate Ubats wherein the U-boat was diverted from its mission as a result of the action, while those in red indicate sinkings. Positions are based — either directly or by extrapolation — on data from various official sources.

While confirmed sinkings were viewed undeniably as victories, it should also be noted that Ubats which concluded with the U-boat returning to base after incurring mission-debilitating damage — or even seeking assistance at sea with wounded aboard — were very real victories as well. The boat could be taken out of the fight for weeks or months. Or even worse, sunk while exposed on the surface seeking assistance, as in the case of U-422.

In lieu of an actual attack, the constant ASW activity also forced boats under. There are many documented cases of commanders aborting the shot, or the positioning to shoot at the last minute due to aircraft being detected overhead. U-106, for example, would have surely come away from the St. Lawrence with more then just one (the SS Waterton) sinking had it not been for EAC's persistent patrolling. They had had many targets in the crosshairs. Her commander's war diary for that particular patrol is full of allusion to frustration due to air activity.

u/k = unknown, c/w = crew wounded, c/wd =crew wounded and dead, n/d = no damage, m/d = minor damage, h/d = heavy damage, Ubat = U-boat Attack, RTB = Return To Base, MV = Merchant Vessel, USN = United States Navy.

Map	Page	Aircraft	U-boat	Date	Result	Note
1	4	Catalina	u/k	23/07/41	u/k	Ubat but U-boat not named
2	7		U-106	11/10/42	>>	SS Waterton Sunk, no Ubat
3	16	Sunderland	U-281	17/10/43	3 c/w	aircraft lost; U-448 RTB
			U-448		c/wd	with 1 dead & 2 wounded
4			U-648	20/11/43	n/d	aircraft lost
5			U-625	10/03/44	sunk	no survivors
6	18	Hurricane	U-513	05/09/42	>>	2 MV sunk, no Ubat
			U-518	02/11/42	>>	2 MV sunk, no Ubat
7	20	Bolingbroke	U-754	23/03/42	m/d	continued patrol
8	36	Digby	U-520	30/10/42	sunk	no survivors

Map	Page	Aircraft	U-boat	Date	Result	Note
9	36	Liberator	U-420	03/07/43	h/dc/w	RTB, 2 dead, 1 wounded
10			U-889	15/05/45	>>	U-boat surrendered
11			U-341	19/09/43	sunk	no survivors
12			U-270	22/09/43	h/d	RTB due to hull damage
13	37		U-377	22/09/43	c/w	RTB with wounded cmdr.
14			U-275	22/09/43	n/d	continued patrol
15			U-402	22/09/43	n/d	continued patrol
16			U-422	23/09/43	3 c/w	RTB, sunk enroute by USN
17			U-420	26/10/43	sunk	no survivors
18	54	Lysander	U-96	23/02/42	m/d	continued patrol
19	62	Hudson	U-658	30/10/42	sunk	no survivors
20			U-521	31/10/42	m/d	continued patrol
21			U-69	21/10/42	n/d	continued patrol
22			U-754	31/07/42	sunk	no survivors

Index